Letters from a Phoenix to a Sparrow
Volume 1

Alpha Mateo

Copyright Notice

Acknowledgements

Thank you to my love, heart, and soul for deciding to love me in the face of so much opposition and continuously inspiring me now and likely until this body draws its last breath.

Thank you to my brother for supporting me as best as he could, not judging, and having the capacity to see the world outside the norms of society and even outside his own perspective.

I also want to thank my daughter for playing the game every day and loving as purely as we are meant to.

Introduction

These are real letters written by a real man to a real woman somewhere in the world. The names and some details have been changed to protect the privacy of those people.

Characters

Author: Mike/Michael
Michael's siblings: Anthony, Elena, Jessica, and Lisa
Michael's daughter: Daniella
Michael's estranged spouse: Kristen
Michael's lover: Barbara
Barbara's husband: David
Barbara's children: Victor and Karen
Kristen's lover: Jeff
Elena's husband: Greg
Michael's friend: Jason
Michael's ex-girlfriend: Stacy
Kristen's friends: Barbara, Angela

2/11/2022

My Love,

Today is Friday, the day of the week, the second time we saw
each other when we walked in the park. My head is spinning with
confusion, pain, and sadness. Whenever I feel I am closer to
understanding your choice, I find a problem with my assessment.
Right now, I believe that your deepest desire is to have a happy
family, the picture of a family you didn't have when you were a
child. It breaks my heart to know you believe you are more likely
to get that picture without the love of your life. For you, a family
is more important than your friendship with Kristen and more
important than sharing a life with your soulmate, and you believe
that you couldn't have that picture of a happy family with me.
You feel like you have to choose between those two things, and
you chose to try to create that picture of a family with the father
of your children rather than your soulmate. You are truly setting a
precedent for your children about what is important—to protect
the original family unit at all costs.

You paid that cost, and so have I, so has Kristen, and so will your
children and our children's friendships. You will protect your
original family unit for now, and at the end of your life, you will
look back on your decision and wonder if it was the right choice.
For your sake, I hope you do feel that way, but I do not believe
you will.

If the day comes any sooner, I will be here. I will forgive you, and
we will make a happy family together.

Yours Forever,
-Mike

2/13/2022

My Love,

It's Sunday, but I thought my next letter to you would be on
Friday. I don't know what I'm doing. I don't know if you'll ever
even read this. Who am I talking to, really? Maybe a ghost. Maybe
myself. I was very hurt and frustrated by you telling me to email
you at work. It made me feel like a piece of garbage. I know you
would have preferred to just cut me off completely, but you were
trying to be nice.

Today, I took Daniella to get her hair done up. As we were sitting
in silence on the car ride back, she told me, "Papa, I miss
Barbara. I missed her so many times." I told her, "I miss her
too." She asked, "Why can we not see her? Mama said we cannot
see Barbara anymore" I told her, "She's really busy, but I think
she misses you too."

Your family would not have been broken if you separated from
David. But now, your family is broken—the family you had with
me, Kristen, Daniella, Karen, and Victor.

Kristen told me about your meeting with Angela. She told me
you told Angela you couldn't reconcile how you felt about me
with the fact that I love Kristen.

I moved out because Kristen couldn't either. I could see a future
with you and not her and vice versa. Neither one would be
painless because I will always love you both, and whoever can
accept that first will spend most of what is left of my life with me.

I realize now you didn't expect our relationship to last forever.
You let me believe it because you didn't want to hurt me. You
saw our love as captured romantically in letters to be appreciated
as something that happened in the past. You knew it was
temporary and tried to make it last as long as possible, but
ultimately, you never planned to spend your life with me.

I hope everything I'm writing is wrong, but even if it's not, I will
welcome you with open arms if I ever see you again. I don't hold

anything against you. This form we take is like a child stuck walking on a bridge between oceans. I hope this life teaches you something that makes the next life we live together one that allows you to value what fate has given, gifted to you.

Your love,
-Mike

Alpha Nagori,

"Why should I not write to you every day?" I asked myself this question this morning, and no answer came.

It was 2:00 am, and I awoke at 1:00 am because I needed to finish some work. I was supposed to do it this weekend, but I couldn't concentrate. My mind is searching for something, and I didn't know what it was until now; it was searching for a way back to you, so my heart could be at ease. I realize now that these letters I am writing you are the only way back to you right now. Maybe they're not for you. Maybe they're for me. Cathartic, if you will. I have spent so much time and energy trying to let you go. I think I'll give up now and accept that I don't need to or want to.

I'm smiling now, imagining you having boxes and boxes of my letters brought to you when you're on your death bed. Sorry, I know that sounds a little morbid.

I hope my love for you and all the joy it can bring you is so much more than a memory. You told me once that "the letters I write you will still exist after we die." I understand that now to mean that you will appreciate our love even after it ends and that you expected it to end. I think you underestimated my heart. You underestimated the infinite aspect of love. It doesn't run out just because I cannot be with you and cannot talk to you. My love for you will never die because it is true love. It is the same love that creates life and binds the universe together.

I also realized and now believe that Daniella is at least partially psychic. In December, out of the blue, she told me, "Papa, if you miss Barbara, you can just drive to her house and see her, ok?" However, I never said anything about you to her, and neither has Kristen.

Today is Valentine's Day. I hoped we would be waking up next to each other on a mountain in Colorado. Hey, maybe we'll get lucky and still do that someday. I bought you a gift, but I guess I'll have to wait to give it to you.

I wanted you just to see it the next time we made love, but since I might be in a coffin the next time you see me, I'll tell you about it here. I did get a tattoo. It's the word "Love," and it's because of you. "Love is a word," I wrote in the letter to you and Kristen. You are that word written on my heart that I cannot remove nor try anymore.

For you, love, our love, exists as a memory, something captured in a letter in November of 2021. For me, it is an active ever-pervasive thing living and growing in my heart. It seems that whether I am with you or not, I will spend the rest of my life living with my love for you in my heart.

But if love, for you, is only something captured in a letter. Let it be captured in these letters if it's not experienced through interaction, touch, and conversation. Let the world know and understand that true love cannot be killed or silenced by a jealous or insecure spouse. It lives in the hearts of those it was given to regardless of the persecution it suffers.

I love you, and I will always do. Nothing and no one will ever take my love for you out of my heart, not even me.

Happy Valentine's Day

-Alpha Mateo

Sparrow,

It's been a week since you told me to email you at work. There's a knot in my stomach still trying to untie itself.

Today seems a little bit easier than yesterday. Kristen seems to be having some breakthroughs. I am so sorry that we weren't ready to receive you into our relationship. I was ready, but she wasn't, and we both were not educated enough. I'm very sorry about the pain she caused you, and I'm sorry for being naïve. I'm sorry that I said, "I don't think you know how to have a relationship." There was a better way to express what I meant. I should have said, "I would rather compromise than you just agree to do what I want and then change your mind."

I slept in today. I have these blackout curtains that block all the light coming into the room; they're really wonderful!

I told Kristen we should ask Angela if she can arrange for you, Victor, Daniella, and Karen to spend some time together. I hope you agree.

It's funny how much of my thoughts are on David now. Somehow, we went from us being concerned I was rescuing you from him to him standing between us. I guess me becoming the villain was inevitable. And my only hope to see you again is he becomes a child of light or a black hole. The grey area between those two things keeps me from you. He holds the key to our family being re-unified because you have given him that power out of pity for him.

The spring is coming, Sparrow, and I do hope your cage is unlocked, so you will be free.

-Phoenix

My heart,

Yesterday, I decided to write a book. It's more of a list, really. I'll try to give you a copy once it's published, and your name will be on it. I would have asked your permission, but there's no way for me to do that right now. Speaking of things I didn't ask your permission for, I printed the picture you sent me of you holding a rose, and it's in my living room. I hope you don't mind.

I recall now when I told you, half-joking, that it would be wonderful to spend Valentine's Day with you and Kristen in Colorado, and you wrote in our group chat, "I don't mind." And you also added, "I love you for this," which I took to mean you praised my sexuality.

There are so many parts of me I want to share and explore with you. And I want to learn and explore every part of you. I miss you so, so, so much—every single part of you.

-Your heart

Darling,

It's pretty early, 4:04 am. Jason and I are on our way to Colorado. I don't remember if I told you we were going skiing. We stopped at a Holiday Inn Express in Amarillo, Texas, so that Jason could sleep. We left early, around 6 pm, so we could try to beat a storm that was coming down yesterday. Then Jason developed a kind of phobia of tornadoes a couple of years ago after a tornado destroyed their neighbors' house. He was very concerned about it. So we stopped when we got to an area near the rain, and I drove through the storm. I reassured him that I grew up in Florida and had driven through many storms before. While we were driving through the rain, I asked him if he felt better that I was driving. He said, "Yes, definitely." I could tell he was at ease but felt a little embarrassed that he was afraid of tornadoes. I could barely see anything, but I remained perfectly calm as the rain poured over the windshield, partly because I had driven in the rain like that before and partly because I knew he needed me to be calm.

I'm pretty tired now; I couldn't sleep. I used to joke that I couldn't sleep in hotel rooms that didn't have paintings on the walls, but this room has paintings. It's more likely due to the fact that I didn't take melatonin and sleep aid like I normally do or the fact that I drank an entire monster energy drink just before we got to the hotel. Jason has insomnia, and he said at the last moment, he couldn't sleep in the car and didn't want to drive all night. So, we stopped.

The wind is blowing loudly outside, and it's snowing. I guess we didn't completely avoid the storm. I recall the window in the hotel where we made love those two times. I pulled the couch in from the other room and put it next to the window. There was a kind of waterfall in the courtyard pool, which my room was next to. The pool was closed, but I wanted to hear the sound of that waterfall because the sound of water reminds me of you. So, I opened the window and sat on that couch for hours and hours, longing to walk across that bridge with you.

The sound of water still reminds me of you—every raindrop brings the memory of you and the hope for a kiss. I was so calm as the rain poured over us also because I felt your love with me. I was ready to be lifted out of the ground by your love like a flower in the desert in the rain or like a car in a tornado driving in the night.

Whether the skies bring snow or rain or are barren and thirsty, I will drive us through it. I will stay calm and reassure you, and you will be at ease. I will keep our love in my heart not as a memory but as something that lives, that longs for us to be together again, that in faith writes to you each day, whatever the weather.

-Mike

2/18/2022

Hey Baby,

How are you doing today? I wish I knew.

We arrived yesterday at the cabin in the mountains. Here, there's a photo of trees in the autumn, and they're yellow against a blue sky with a mountain peeking out just above the trees. Blue and yellow, you wrote in my heart across space and time, so I would not forget you, and I have not.

Stacy reached out to me yesterday. She stopped talking to me at the beginning of January because her husband Diego found out we were talking again. It's like the 10th time in over 8 years. He still doesn't realize he's still married. Poor guy is afraid of losing his wife. I know what that feels like. Anyway, she always comes back to me no matter how many times Diego tells her not to talk to me, but she always will because she knows I will always love her and will never turn her away.

You will also come back to me one day because you know I will always love you and never turn you away. I bought tickets to an Alaskan cruise for September. I was planning to go myself, but I bought a ticket with your name on it for some reason. I don't really think you will go. Obviously, I hope you will, but it was more of an act of faith.

When I told you I wanted to spend the rest of my life with you, I really meant it. I feel like I'm married to you, at least my commitment. Obviously, you're not spending your life with me, but it won't change my desire to.

-Mike

Baby,

This morning was hard. I've been debating on whether or not to
tell you about it because I want my letters to you to give you joy
and hope. I hope my hesitation communicates how much I care
for you and care about how what I say makes you feel.

Jason and I went to a bar/restaurant last night. A cute girl sat
down next to us, so I started talking to her. Suddenly, Jason
walked out of the bar, offended that I wasn't focusing on him
100%. Thankfully, I handled it really well because I already
understood what he was feeling based on my experience with
Kristen.

I've had physical pain in my chest for the last couple of hours. I
feel so alone, aspirationally and now emotionally. No one I know
loves the way I do and what is worse is that my heart offends
people. Who I am is an offense to people.

I wish I could ask you how your day was.

-Mike

Barbara,

If I had to choose between you and Kristen, I would choose you. I hope you never make me choose, but if you did, I would choose you, as long as you chose me too.

Kristen has become very kind and understanding, giving me some energy to think about how I feel about you. This ski trip was supposed to be a relief from all the pain I have been in over the last two-to-three months, but it has just brought me more pain. I love skiing more than anything. Every little bit of joy I have reminds me of the joy you brought me, and I am reminded that my greatest joy in life will only ever be a tiny fraction of the joy you give me.

Every single thing reminds me of you. I got a painful deep tissue massage yesterday, and I was calling out to you in my mind at the most difficult parts.

I'm not trying to be unhappy; it's just the opposite. Joy reminds me of you. Pain reminds me of you. The cold. Water. I wake up in tears almost every day. I want to be positive and hopeful, but some days are harder than others. Trying to forget you feels like a betrayal of myself. So, I'm starting to realize this just may be the way the rest of my life will be. You are a part of me that is missing, a part I found and lost again. There is a hole inside me, and I know now that no one but you will ever be able to fill that hole.

-Mike

2/21/2022

Hey Baby,

Sorry if my handwriting is a little messed up. Yesterday, I broke my clavicle (on my left side) skiing. At least I can still write. I feel like it was a near-death experience. I suddenly became lighthearted. I feel like I shouldn't take life so seriously all the time because it can end as early as we want or later than we want, and it will come to an end with or without our help.

I see the sun shining over the horizon of a mountain as the cold air rushes towards me. You are that cold air released by the night, waiting on top of the mountain looking for me. The sun is time. I feel more confident now than I ever have. I am very confident now, more than I ever have been, that I am running to you, you to me, and we are on the same path at different ends.

I love you so much. Keep running, and you will reach me.

-Mike

Love,

This morning was interesting. Daniella threw a temper tantrum which caused Kristen to throw a temper tantrum. Kristen turned facedown my pictures of you, her, and Stacy, and she said she couldn't come to my house anymore because it was a shrine to her failure.

Fun day.

Every time I am optimistic about my relationship with Kristen, it blows up. I'm fine with my life being like this for now. Fate will not let me suffer long if I am cheerful despite the pain.

I love you.

-Mike

Baby,

I'm awake early again today. I have lost some peace I regained because of what Kristen did yesterday, but I still feel optimistic about things.

I started seeing a new therapist, and she is polyamorous too. She is not intimidated by my sexual appetite like my last therapist was. I think my conversations with her are giving me a sense of emotional safety that I no longer have with Kristen, who really is bad for my psychological health. It's so clear for me to see that now. Every time I start to do better, she does or says something to bring me down. She said I built a shrine to you in this house. The only thing I have built a shrine to is myself and love, and you are part of me. The poems I wrote to you are on the walls. Paintings I made for you and you made for me are on the walls. I asked Kristen for paintings, but she never gave them.

I don't remember if I told you that I asked her to go to Paris with me. But she told me she didn't want to go with me because I might get depressed and ruin her dream. She weaponizes my vulnerabilities against me. You are right to believe she doesn't deserve me.

If I am honest, no one should be treated how she treats me. Everyone deserves love.

I broke up with her again. I don't trust her to even come inside my house. I think this is how she wants things to be anyway; she is just afraid to tell me.

I'm sorry I made the wrong choice. I should have picked you. I just didn't know how to.

I love you.

-Mike

Barbara,

This morning, Russia invaded Ukraine. It reminded me of something I wrote when we sent you money. I wrote:

> The enlightened can neither give nor receive, for they own nothing

How is it connected? Lol, I know, right? Russia, or Putin really, is trying to take ownership of something he wants to possess.

I really believe for others to find the celestial love we found, the love that can never start a war, they have to give up the belief that things can be owned. If things cannot be owned, they cannot be taken, so I do not feel you were taken from me. But David probably feels I was trying to take you from him, and you were trying to take me from Kristen. He believes in ownership, but we do not.

While I know you have chosen to be away from me, I do not feel I lost you because I do not believe I owned you, had you, or possessed you.

At one point, I didn't know where you were, but I now know you are on the same road as me, walking towards me. You are on the same road as me but on the other side, so our experiences and choices look different.

I miss your letters. I know you don't send them because you promised David not to talk to me or think it will help me forget you. But Alpha Nagori, Baby, I will never forget you. I will never give up trying to find my way back to you. I know where you are now; I just have to keep walking, loving you, writing, and believing I will one day see you again.

And so I will.

-Mike

Baby,

I had a dream about you last night. I was in the house I grew up
in when you, David, your kids, your mother, and your
grandmother came over. I had just finished writing you a letter
and was surprised to see you all. Suddenly, your grandmother
walked up to me, grabbed my crotch, and gave me a smile. While
I was distracted, she took the letter I wrote you. As I began to
search for the letter, you confronted me. I could tell you were
very angry at me. You felt like I took advantage of you and was
using you.

I hope that dream is just my subconscious trying to guess how
you feel.

Yesterday, I realized an issue in Kristen and I's relationship and
why she is possessive only when we are sleeping together. She
believes sex is an exchange between two people, each giving and
receiving. Giving a part of yourself and receiving a part of
someone else.

When you give and don't want to, it's a sacrifice. When you give a
part of yourself you don't want to, a part of you is taken, and a
part of you is lost. When you give a part of yourself enough
times, you lose yourself. When you give more than you receive,
something is owed to you. You are entitled to a certain status and
treatment. You are allowed to be resentful for what was taken.
You are allowed to be mean and are entitled to forgiveness so
that the exchange is fair. That person belongs to you until their
debt is repaid. They owe you. Of course, nothing can be given,
taken, lost, received, or owed if nothing is owned. I'm convinced
now that love and ownership are enemies, and wherever they co-
exist, so does conflict.

I'm sorry you may not be able to see your mother until the Russia
and Ukraine conflict is resolved.

I love you, and I miss you so much.

-Mike

2/26/2022

My Soul,

Yesterday evening, I had a thought appear in my head. Kristen had secretly orchestrated for us to see each other. You were walking towards me on the sidewalk from the road to my front door. There was no hesitation in you, no doubt, no fear, no anger—only happiness and excitement. When I saw you, I froze, checking to see if my mind was deceiving me or if my faith had delivered you to me. I got the sense that our time was limited, but I didn't let it take away any of the joy from the moment. Your hair was a little bit longer than the last time I saw you. You were wearing a white dress with flowers and a grey knitted sweater which was not buttoned up. Your hair was naturally brown but with black highlights, and your legs were kept warm with grey stockings. In your ears, you wore the origami earrings you wore on the first night we fell asleep together. You stopped and stood still when you saw me, placing your black boots and legs together. It was dark outside, but the starlight and moonlight seemed to shine through you, and then your smile, oh, your smile broke down every part of sadness in me. Yet somehow, I still stood there wondering at your beauty and the energy of your presence with tears of relief and joy crawling down my cheeks. My arms were fully ready to wrap around you like a phoenix wraps its wings around a sparrow, my heart yearning and burning inside for you. Then I opened my eyes, and you were not there.

I usually write to you first thing in the morning because you are the first thought in my mind each day, and I cannot wait to share my heart with you—everything that happened since yesterday and how my love for you has grown since then. Now I will keep the letter open and write to you all day long and close the letter before I go to sleep.

Kyiv survived the night. Many thought it would fall. I am still in a lot of pain, and the painkillers I am taking make me kind of drowsy. C.B.D is definitely helping.

Kristen was supposed to go to Vegas with Angela for her birthday, but the ice storm delayed the flight, and she realized I needed help. Our relationship is such a roller coaster. I really hope she is learning and growing. I couldn't even take a shower, so she helped me wash myself. Last night, she asked if I "wanted to have no strings attached sex," which I took to mean she realized she had been expecting something in return for having sex with me and no longer wanted to do that. I only hope it is true and that it lasts.

I'm about 80% done with my book, although I need to focus on work as I am really lagging behind.

I really love that I can write you these letters and no one can stop me. Nobody's fear can keep me from loving you.

Last night after I had that vision of you, I went into my bedroom and started to cry. Kristen and I were watching 20,000 Leagues Under the Sea (1954), so she noticed I went missing. She came into the bedroom and saw I was crying. She got on her knees as I sat on the bed. Then she held my hands and asked if I was crying because I missed you. Sobbingly, I told her yes. Then she began to kiss the tears from my face as if to take away my sadness but to love the part of me that is you. With every kiss, her lips soaked up a little bit of you. And with every part of you, she captured in her kisses of you; she missed you a little bit more too. At one point, I was afraid to cry for you because it was the reason she threw the dishes at me. At least last night, I was a little less afraid and a little more hopeful she will or does accept my love for you.

I had another dream of you and David. In that dream, I was pleading with David to believe us when we thought your relationship with him was completely over, and I was begging him to allow us to see each other. He didn't listen.

I saw that you were on Telegram in the last 48 hours. It says "Last seen recently" when you logged in within the last 48 hours. When I saw that, I had an irresistible urge to let you know I am still with you, so I sent you a message "I am still here, my love." I hope you saw it.

It's been a very tiring day though I didn't do anything. I didn't do any work. I hope you had a good day.

-Mike

I need hope. But hope for what? Hope to be ready physically, mentally, and financially for the day you return to me. "I will build you a garden with flowers of every kind," I wrote you, but I cannot build any kind of garden in this state. So, I will make this my new goal: to build you a garden.

Barbara Gardens

2/27/2022

Barbara,

I fell asleep last night to news about Ukraine and woke up to it
playing. Yesterday began an urge in me to go to Ukraine and
fight. Impossible, obviously, but in my heart echo these words
over and over:

> It is better to die a hero to one person than to live a
> coward to yourself.

Only we know the battles we ran away from. Only we know the
oppressors we surrendered to. Acts of cowardice are rarely seen,
but acts of courage are seen often, and even when they fail, those
courageous are admired because so many want to overcome their
fear, but so few do. Fear is never overcome by the courageous,
for they simply fear something else more. A mother or father
jumps in front of a car to save their child because they fear living
without their child more than they fear dying. So, it's more
accurate to say we have different fears than to say we are
courageous.

Right now, I fear living day after day for the rest of this life apart
from you. So if there was a battle where I could be a hero to at
least one person, I would gladly die to fight it.

When we are in pain, we think about what matters most. When I
got in my first motorcycle accident, I thought about Melanie, my
fourth love. She came to see me in the hospital. When I got my
tattoo, all I could see was your face. When I was lying in the
snow, unable to move at the top of the mountain, all I could see
was your face. I know now that when I die in those brief
moments just before, I will also see your face if I am granted a
brief moment.

You are with me always, and I am with you. It's too bad Russians
prefer a tragedy to a happy ending.

-Mike

Barbara,

As I pulled your mail from the mailbox, a thousand stars danced inside my heart. An upbeat song by Jan Blomquist, "Time Again," plays in the background. A sense of victory fills my soul. Waves of tiny mountains flow over my skin from the top of my head to the tips of my toes. "Love has won the war," every living thing echoes. The dawn has gone, and there is only light wherever I can see.

I know now that absolutely nothing can destroy our love. It is real, and it is alive. Without any request or other communication, we bare our souls to one another. There is no darkness dark enough to drown our love. Oh, glorious night, break now, for our love has survived you and the fire.

-Michael

My Light,

This morning, Daniella fell from a chair and split open the skin
above her eye. Immediately, I called Kristen to come over, and
we took her to get stitches. Doctors wouldn't stitch her because
she was throwing a temper tantrum. I guess she was upset about
something. Eventually, she needed to use the restroom. So I held
her hand and walked her from the car where we were waiting
under the siege of her outburst back into the E.R. I walked to the
grocery store to buy her five "pink balloons," including a
"unicorn" balloon as she requested. After an hour of waiting in
the E.R., Daniella said she wanted to see the doctor, but I guess
the doctor gave up on us. We waited another thirty minutes and
then just went home, to my house.

I made the mistake of telling Kristen how happy I was about the
letters you sent. She complained that she was writing me a letter
but now didn't want to give it to me because she didn't want to
compete with you. Also, she said she was upset that you didn't
write her letters. In other words, she couldn't be more unhappy
about the happiness you brought me. Ultimately, it led to me
telling her some hard things for her to hear. I really don't believe
she will ever change. She will try to steal my happiness in any way
she can. She has been doing this for many years; it's just very
obvious now.

Right now, she is in too much pain for me to share any kind of
life with. I wish I could have known sooner she would turn out
this way, but I guess seeing myself trying is part of the process of
letting her go.

So much hope is in my heart now, and that hope comes from
your love.

-Mike

Barbara,

It seems you are my confidant now. Something I never expected
when I first started talking to you, but it feels so right for this to
be true, ignoring everything else.

I believe I have just begun a journey of acceptance of the end of
my time with Kristen. I know that I love her, but I realize now
more than ever that most people are incapable of change. She
cannot change into someone who can celebrate who I am. I'm
afraid you have learned this sooner than I have.

I am afraid, but there is also so much joy and light in my heart,
and that light is your love for me and my love for you. No one's
fear can drown, destroy, or hide our love, not even our fear.

I do not know the day I will see you again, but I know that day
will come, and knowing this fills my heart and my hope for the
future. I will love and feel joy. I feel so blessed to have found this
love with you, even if I cannot practice it right now.

I love you with all my heart.

-Mike

My Friend,

The only thing worse than being alone is being with someone that makes you feel more alone when you're with them.

   I will let the silence keep me company, and my own voice will lift me out of the darkness.

The words in your letter stuck with me. "To find joy after loss is not my culture." I found it interesting after I recently wrote, "It's too bad Russians prefer a tragedy to a happy ending." While slightly tongue in cheek, I know that culture is a powerful force.

I find it so inspiring that you have a mind open enough to leave behind elements of your native religion that didn't serve you, and I know you can do the same with culture. There were many days when I thought you chose this path because you preferred a tragedy to a happy ending, but your letter from 2/8 has given me hope that you can overcome it even if you have done so. I believe now that you want to live happily ever after and that you can grow into the person that can find that happiness.

I have a painting I made, a set of triangles that wrap around each other: one side red, another violet, and another blue and yellow. I tried so many times to figure out how exactly things would turn out. Things I hoped for may still come to pass. I recall the poem in the book you showed me with the naked people dancing. I think people and relationships are too complex for me to predict. I see now that this time is meant for all four of us to see that our relationships now do not bring happiness into any of our lives. The only relationship that I believe brings happiness is yours and mine between you and me. And it only brings happiness to you and me. To Kristen and David, it brings pain and sadness. This time, I think, is about all of us letting go of those old relationships. I cannot say what will come after that, but I believe it will be something beautiful.

Our love is like a tree. The dead branches fall off slowly.

-Your Friend

Darling,

I guess I'm writing to you twice a day now ☺.

You are so much a part of my life right now. I know it sounds crazy, but it's true. When I dance, you are dancing with me. When I smile, I'm thinking of you. I don't know what changed. I think Kristen was taking up so much space in my heart, and when I let her go, it was so liberating. And now there is only you, and you only bring me joy.

I have an idea for the title of our first book, "Letters of a Phoenix and a Sparrow." Even as I write the title, chills run down my spine; I feel good.

My love, Barbara, I feel so much in love with you right now. I thought I lost you, but I did not. My love burns so hotly and bright for you right now as if you were with me right now. I can feel your icy fingertips run across my spine as my heartbeat dances rhythmically with yours and my fiery passion for you envelops both like a sparrow wrapped in the wings of a phoenix.

Oh, how much more faith in our love you must have to write me without any of my letters. I know somehow that this faith you show is part of your journey, path, and finding your way back to me.

> Oh, glorious day
> What strength you show to keep back the night
> You stretch out your arms upon me
> Your presence gives color to everything in sight
>
> Oh, glorious day
> What strength you show to lift up the dawn
> You push back the darkness
> Your children dance in raindrops, each one singing your song
>
> Oh, glorious day!
> Look how much love you bring!
> Yesterday you have forgotten
> You brought her back, my love, can finally sing

Oh, glorious day!
Let the pitch of my scream turn into laughter
What has died helps grow something for tomorrow
You are with me, and that means we are together

Oh, glorious day
How you make starlight into the sunlight
Rays of joy and hope burst from my heart
I am with you, against the fearful our faith will fight

.*

                                                        -Mike

Good morning my love!

I feel my desire for you growing so strong; the fabric of space and time evaporates to bring us together as if the laws of physics could not keep us apart. I feel your presence so vibrant with me. I do not believe even God would be able to keep us apart forever, nor would he want to, for together we are Love. We are God. My God! I don't know what is happening. I feel like I can feel your body lying on top of mine right now. If it didn't feel so good, it would be overwhelming.

It's about 8:30 am. I imagine you have already arrived at work. Your hair is a little bit longer but not quite as long as in the painting you sent me. Maybe I have just finally lost it. Maybe I'm becoming delusional, but I can feel you sitting next to me now. Kristen says I just have fantasies, imagination, and illusions, but I don't believe that right now. Sometimes I think our love is imaginary, but really, Kristen just hasn't accepted that it is real, and she tries to persuade me it was a mirage.

I'm sorry it took me so long to get here. I really hoped she would come around.

I only want you now, and you are the only one I want to be with right now, and I feel the beauty in that exclusivity in my heart. I know it may not always be this way, but right now, it is.

I am yours and yours alone.

-Mike

3/3/2022

Barbara, My Soul,

Today, I had to go to the orthodontist to get my last set of teeth trays. I remember how painful they were and how difficult getting them out was the first day I got them. I remember your words of encouragement. You told me it would be worth it. I believed you, and in retrospect, I see the things I have accomplished have been painful, exhausting, and frustrating. They all took time to deliver benefits, and I believe that loving and loving you will be like this and that I will reap what I am sowing. With each letter I write you, I know I am sowing seeds of love into our hearts, and even though I do not yet see the fruit, I take comfort in knowing I am planting in fertile ground.

Our love is and will be the fruit of our work, pain, and frustration. I told you, "Our love will last," and so it has. Some land is made for building cities and some for growing food, while other lands are meant to be untouched so that nature can thrive on its own. Some hearts were made to build cities, while others were meant to plant and harvest.

Most people and cultures see divorce and separation as a failure and to be avoided. We learn that someone has had many marriages, and we think there is something wrong or broken about that person, but the truth is we are judging them and what is worse by a single data point. Some crops grow and are harvested faster than others. Every field needs rest—a time to be free in nature so that wild untethered growth can occur. Every season is ended by a winter. Why are divorce and separation not celebrated as the end of a successful harvest and the beginning of a new season?

Well, the winter is over, and it is time to till the fields. I sat outside today and let the sun soak deep into my skin. It was so warm and hot. I recall the memory of an image I had about how we would spend the summer at the lake house we stayed at on Halloween. The day after Halloween, when I was absolutely on fire with love for you, I did an experiment on myself. When you take ecstasy, your body is flooded with serotonin. You develop a positive association with everything and everyone you are with. I selected a random set of songs and played them over and over the first week of November. I did this experiment to see if, at least chemically, our love was real. One of those songs was "Lemonade" by Alexandra Stan. It was a summer song at the beginning of the winter, but I still feel so good when I listen to it. I remember the feeling of love I had, and I have right now. My experiment proved that chemically, our love is real, like ecstasy. I didn't know it at the time, but it was a promise I didn't know I needed. A promise the summer would come.

You and I are so attached to nature that we follow the seasons. We have small cycles and large cycles. We make resolutions in the spring, work hard in the summer, harvest our work in the fall and reflect and plan in the winter.

I have reflected and planned. Now, I am tilling my heart. I am preparing my heart and life for your love for me and mine for you. I do not know how long the spring will be, how long I will wait for you to be in my arms, but I know the summer will come. It is a season for you to be loved, and your heart is a fertile field to plant in.

"I will draw the sun," said the artist, "for I am not afraid of its power and love."

-Mike

Barbara,

A cool breeze glides gently over me, its fingertips rustling the leaves and the emotion on my soul. A tear, alone, begins a short journey from my eye.

I don't know why but I decided to google your name today. Maybe I wanted to see if there was anything I could learn about you. I must admit it felt stalkerish, but something tells me you wouldn't mind. Behold, at least I think, I found a photo of you on your work website. I think it is recent because your hair is a little longer, and your figure is still mouthwatering. I studied your face like I studied your body that Sunday afternoon. Your eyes are filled with so much sadness, not the kind of sadness that has broken you but one that has made you stronger. Like carbon molecules under pressure, your spirit shines like a Diamond. You have a sense of clarity and endurance in your eyes. I see great sorrow in your eyes but sorrow that is being overcome, making you stronger, even more unbreakable.

I set the picture as my phone background. I hope that's not too creepy. I would ask you for a newer photo, but I cannot. I get the sense that you and David need to have zero contact with me so you can be confident your incompatibility has nothing to do with my influence. So, I won't contact you.

I think about the words in my letter, "Your heart is a fertile field to plant in." The gravity of the truth in those words pulls that solitary tear down my cheek like a meteor crashing into earth.

-Phoenix

Barbara,

Each day I wake up now, I am excited a new day has come because it is a new day, another day I get to confess my love to you. I know my love is a life spring to your heart, and with each letter, I drop and drip joy into the garden that is your soul.

The best I can do now to share my love for you with others is to share my writing, and oh, how much I want to tell the world that I love you. How much I want to tell them you are kind. How much I want to tell them you are beautiful and strong. Ten-thousand chariots are tethered to my heart to stop me from running to you right now. How I yearn to tell people about you, that you are faithful and just, that your courage and perseverance can move mountains, that mothers celebrate your intuition with children. Your solidarity and peace could be the foundation of cities, and your steadfast spirit and commitment are the foundation for skyscrapers. Your determined tranquility is a steady wind in the sails of all blessed to be a part of your life. Oh, how much I long to be in your presence.

> You are the wind unto my sail
>> Your love moves my fleet
> You are the water of my soul
>> Your kindness as deep as the sea

> Wherever your heart blows
>> My ship will follow
> I am the captain of your soul
>> And you are the first mate today and tomorrow

-Mike

Barbara,

It's lunchtime now. I thought writing to you once a day would be enough, but it seems to be going the other direction. Writing to you makes me feel good because I know you will appreciate every letter I write.

I was re-reading your February 8th letter; I think it's my favorite letter now. At the bottom, the word "Buddhism" stands out. I recall a girlfriend, Yolanda, I had was Buddhist, and I broke up with her because of that; I was Christian. Recently, I went through a mixed collection of letters between Kristen and me. I found two letters Yolanda wrote me; she wrote them after we broke up. In retrospect, she was the kindest girl I dated. I do think there is some connection between inner peace, kindness, and Buddhism.

And sorry, I realized after I found those letters that you were not the first person to write me a letter. I also found two letters from Stacy, one apology letter from Kristen, and a card Kristen gave me on the Valentine's Day I proposed to her.

I hope the volume of letters I am writing you doesn't diminish the value of each letter.

Last night, I had a nightmare that Kristen had turned her back on me and was seeing someone else. I was so distraught that I woke up yelling, "No! No!" I know our path is the right one, but the attachment is, in my opinion, unfortunately still there. It's not an attachment that will easily break. Maybe Buddhism can help.

Daniella spends every day with me now. She doesn't want to be around Kristen because she has so much bitterness and anger inside her and takes it out on Daniella. Her hair is so much work; I can see how it would feel empowering to keep your hair short for a while so that having long hair felt more like a choice than an expectation. She loves how I do her hair, and she seems to get a new sense of joy in her each time I do it. I think she even looks forward to it because it feels like affection rather than the pain she is used to from Kristen.

I keep imagining you showing up on my doorstep one day, fully packed, ready to start your life with me. Ready to leave all the pain and sorrow of your old life behind. I imagine how you will wake up with me some days and do Daniella's hair and how she will enjoy it and love you. I imagine the kids playing in the big backyard I have as we share champagne on a cool day. And I take a breath in and out, knowing that I get closer to that day with each day that passes.

I miss you so much.

-Mike

3/4/2022

Barbara,

Do you remember when I told you that I felt the entire universe, every blade of grass, every tree, every footstep taken by every person was designed so that we could be together? I still believe that, and wow, I definitely did not expect things to unfold the way they have. However, they must be part of that design because I believe we have followed our hearts, and somehow this period of separation is part of our destiny to love each other, prove to each other and the world that our love is the purest and truest love.

It's been one month since you read my last letter at the time I am writing this. By the time you are reading this, I hope it is obvious that I will never give up on loving you.

I love you, Barbara. Good night.

Yours Truly,
-Mike

3/5/2022

Friend,

This morning, Daniella woke me up when she came to me on the couch where I was sleeping. I sleep on the couch many nights. It's harder to realize I'm alone on the couch.

Stacy told me about the movie "Love in the Time of Cholera." She said it reminded her of her and me. I read the Wikipedia summary; then I laid on the floor crying. I didn't think it reminded me of Stacy and me. I thought it reminded me of you and me. As I was lying on the floor crying last night, I asked myself, "If I am so loved, why am I alone right now?" Maybe ironically, I was listening to the song that answered that question, *Father Ocean (Ben Böhmer remix)* by Monolink.

>   We can only see the deepest desires of our soul when we are alone in the silence of our hearts.

The deepest desire of my soul isn't to be not alone but to be with my childhood friend, the one I have lived eight-hundred lives with, you. You are that friend I was missing growing up. You are that friend I have been searching for even though I didn't realize it. You are that friend I have waited for my whole life to be with. When I am alone in the silence, I only think of you. When I smile, I am thinking of you. When I am in pain, I think of you. When the hurricane of life passes over me, I am holding onto you. I cried because I don't want to wait my whole life to see you again. I want to live the rest of my life with you, not wait the rest of my life for you. I don't care what movies have been made or what psychological condition I have. I know who you are. You are my Alpha Nagori. My friend across time.

-Mike
Your Friend

Barbara,

I have come to the point in my relationship with Kristen where I realize I cannot help her anymore. Daniella doesn't want to see or talk to her. Kristen thinks Daniella doesn't want to spend time or talk to her because they don't spend time or talk. On Friday, Kristen asked to pick up Daniella from school, and we previously agreed Daniella would stay with Kristen on Tuesday and Friday. Last week, she didn't want to stay with her on Tuesday, and Friday was no different. I told Kristen she could come over and spend time with Daniella. Fifteen minutes after she arrived, they were quarreling. I asked what was going on, and Kristen just said, "I want to leave." I said, "go." When she tried to leave, Daniella was holding onto her leg, asking her to stay. I could tell Kristen was not in the right emotional state to have a positive interaction. We both knew that. So, I turned on cartoons on the iPad so Daniella would let go of her leg. She did, and then Kristen left. I understand Daniella's behavior. She feels torn because the person supposed to keep her safe and who loves her is also hurting her. I have this same issue with Kristen. Now that I do not live with her, I can see just how mean she is. Her energy is so toxic, and I even feel guilty for supporting her in her treatment of Daniella for the past couple of years. Kristen was a wonderful mother up until she stopped nursing. After that, she grew progressively crueler and more controlling, and I couldn't even realize it because she treated me like that too. I think I am partly to blame. I think I gave Kristen misguided advice on how to interact with her. Maybe I was even mistreating Daniella. Before you loved me, I was very angry because I hated myself and didn't think I had any value. I believe Kristen is in the same situation. I have tried so hard to make her feel valued, but I just don't know how. I'm finally ok with that. Someone else has to make her believe in her worth. I don't have that role right now. I wanted to, but I don't. Anyways this is what is on my mind at the moment.

I also wanted to tell you about a sensation I had last night. I took ecstasy to gain some clarity about how to handle this dilemma with Daniella and Kristen but also spent a little bit of time thinking about you. I felt that some of my recent letters may have been a little obsessive, and I'm sorry if it felt that way and was off-putting. I also felt that, yet again, I need to let you go. These cycles going from a strong commitment to dismissive avoidance are exhausting. I have an insecure attachment style because of the way I was raised. My attachment to Kristen was chaotic but secured most of the time. However, when she hurt me, I became dismissive. With each letter you write me, I become more secure in your love, but I have these really primal instincts to avoid situations and people that make me doubt whether or not they love me. Please give me grace, my love. Objectively, I think considering the circumstances of our relationship or whatever this interaction between us is, it is fair for me to have doubts. Hope isn't a belief that something absolutely will happen but a belief that something can happen. Even though on some days I have doubts, and on other days I am absolutely sure I will see you again, I write to you anyways. This action, even in the face of doubt, is faith. Like courage isn't an absence of fear but rather action despite the fear, true faith takes action despite doubt. You could also say I am in denial that our relationship is over, and according to society's standards and expectations, you would likely be right. The love I have for you is considered an abomination by most people. The first interracial marriage was also thought about this way. The hard part about leading is that initially, you are always alone. Unfortunately for me, I don't often prioritize society's expectations, which has frequently left me isolated. I feel this isolation now in loving you. The only person that celebrates my love for you is Daniella. Yesterday, she saw your picture on my phone and said with some excitement, "That's really nice!" Anthony is supportive, but I wouldn't say he celebrates it. He is monogamous, so he doesn't fully understand how I can simultaneously love more than one person.

Even in the face of all the world's apparent resistance, I still love you and will still write to you because I believe now that my heart is beautiful, and this consistency in love for you is beautiful, even if no one else thinks so.

Even if you told me you hated me, I would still love you because my love is a choice, and that choice is not affected by the coming and goings of life. It survives through all seasons, in good times and bad, for better or worse, and even after death in this life.

Yours Always,
-Mike

Barbara,

Daniella has figured out that I write letters to you every day. I never told her I was writing letters to anyone. I'm writing this letter now because she told me, "Papa, can you write a letter?" I asked, "Who should I write a letter to?" She walked over to your picture, picked it up, and pointed to it. I asked why I should write you a letter, and she said, "Because you do that every day, because that's really nice."

I don't know if I told you this, but I think she has some telepathic link with me. One time in December, out of the blue, she told me, "Papa, you know if you miss Barbara, you can just drive to her house to see her." A couple of days ago, she asked me, "Papa, why does mama not want Barbara to come live with you?" Again, I never said anything about it. Maybe Kristen is talking to her; I don't know.

We just made popcorn. It was flying everywhere out of the popcorn maker. Daniella was hysterical with laughter. There is so much joy, peace, and love in this house, and it causes me a lot of pain to accept that the path to this joy was to remove Kristen from our lives. I really hope she finds the joy we have found without her. Knowing I did everything I could to try to keep her a part of the family gives me peace. And you know Barbara, keeping an unhappy family together is not better than having part of the family happy. People make their own choices, adults, I mean. Children don't get to choose their circumstances. Adults sometimes don't have control over their circumstances, like the families fleeing Ukraine right now. But I did have a choice, and it took popcorn flying all over the kitchen to realize I had made the right choice. Even though Daniella knows I'm sad sometimes, she feels <u>safe</u>. I really underestimated the importance and value of emotional safety. The strangest thing is I actually felt safe when I was living with Kristen. Granted, I still think she provided some safety; she actually used those vulnerable moments I had with her against me over the long run. The only real way I could see things clearly was to live apart from her. There was no other way.

I hope you can provide clarity to your life and enough safety for your children to allow them to be happy.

-Mike

Barbara,

I woke up this morning with a sense of determination to focus on work. This was shortly followed by a sense of feeling overwhelmed, followed by a brief craving to smoke. It's been more than two weeks since I smoked, so I don't want to ruin my streak. For the last couple of days, I have been watching the news on Ukraine, and frankly, I am petrified by the images of death and sadness. I woke up thinking that regardless of what was going on in my life and in the world, I couldn't let it debilitate me from being responsible or working towards my goals. I was supposed to work on the weekend but didn't, and now I'm behind again. I am actually not used to watching Daniella the entire weekend. Right now, I feel like a single dad. I can't keep up with the housework because of my broken clavicle. Even hanging up a towel is exhausting. While the suffering of the Ukrainian people continues to break my heart, I hope that their example of resolve and courage inspires me to find in myself a renewed sense of determination and courage to overcome my shortcomings, setbacks, and weaknesses.

I spend a lot of time thinking, and sometimes I wonder if that's helpful or hurtful. Am I giving myself space to grieve, or am I drowning in self-pity?

Even with the setback of breaking my clavicle, I accomplished the most important goal for me: to stop smoking. I hoped to start a new routine which would include working out, but that will have to be put on hold. It seems like the only thing consistent in my life right now is the letters I write to you. I know you may feel like I am writing these letters more as a coping tool. I must admit that is a possibility. But when I write them, I am meditating on you. These letters are written to you. Even though sometimes I feel I am writing to the void, most of the time, my heart is communicating to you, my Barbara, my friend. I don't feel like these letters are a journal, especially since I also keep a journal. These letters are an expression of my longing and desire to have communion with you, to, in the only way I can, share my heart and my life with you. But they can never be a substitute for you.

God, I miss you so much. As I write this, tears fall from my face. To be honest, I don't want to write you letters every day. I want to have a conversation with you. I don't want to check the mailbox every day, hoping I might get a letter from you so I can learn something about your life. Sometimes, I am afraid that you will not want these letters when I see you again because you have moved on.

But I don't want you to feel suffocated or encumbered by me. I have always found it such a hard line to walk. I did feel safe to give you all of my heart because that is who I am; I am so ready to trust someone not to hurt me, not to reject me. If you ever want that person to be you, I will be happy about it.

With all my heart.

-Your Mike

3/7/2022

Barbara,

The world is different from what it was seventy years ago. Those
Disney fairy tales offer an idea of an ideal monogamous
relationship. For thousands of years, cultures had been slowly
gravitating towards monogamy. They say a story has a happy
ending if you end it when its happy. All of our stories about love
start and end in the same way. Technology changes how we
interact. For the first time in thousands of years, we can interact
with people on the other side of the world. Cultures are blending
at a faster rate than ever before. The nature of our relationships
and the development of our relationships are changing, so the
nature of our love stories is changing. We are at the very early
stages of a shift in our love stories that are being catapulted by
technology. Our love stories are dynamic, a mixture of old love
stories, monogamy, individual freedom, personal growth, sexual
exploration, and self-actualization. Society and individual rights
are more complex and fluidic. What we need today isn't what we
needed ten years ago, and we have the resources and social
structures to adapt our lives to what we need as we change and
grow.

I don't know that you will be the most important need I have for
the rest of my life. But I am absolutely confident you are what I
need now, and I believe I am what you need right now.

Kristen was what I needed eleven years ago. She is not what I
need anymore, and I may not be what she needs anymore. She
will change into something new over the next six months, and so
will I.

I don't believe our story is over because we did not have a happy
ending.

I'll see you soon.

-Mike

3/8/2022

My Love,

Good morning! And Happy Women's Day!

Ok, maybe the exclamations were a bit much since I haven't had all my coffee yet.

I woke up with a song playing in my head: *Ocean Avenue* by Yellowcard. The words "If I could find you now, things would get better" echo in my head repeatedly. It was a song I listened to in high school. It's a torturous melody, and even though I relate with the lyrics right now, I don't want that song in my head. It reminded me of a period of my life when I was very lonely, very heartbroken, bouncing from one crush to the next and somewhere in between committing attempted suicide. I hated this period of my life, the emotional turmoil it created, the constant disappointment. It didn't end until I went to the boot camp.

I wish I could find a way to throw myself into my work now, distract myself until you come back to me. I know you love me and always will, but I don't know if you will return to me. All the advice I have read online tells me that we should do what we're doing now. I need at least six months to grieve the loss of my relationship with Kristen. Maybe more like twelve due to how long it was, which obviously brings me to another question: are you and David grieving the loss of your relationship as well, or have you found a renewed, fruitful marriage? I guess I'm not meant to know, and probably your therapist advised you that interacting with me was interfering with your grieving process. And why couldn't you tell me this? Maybe you weren't sure if you would stay with David or not and didn't want to get my hopes up. Well, I'm laughing now because whether or not you separate from David, my hope will always be to be with you in any way possible, friends, lovers, pen-pals ☺. God, I don't really want to be your pen pal or just friend, but I would take it. You said you don't believe in becoming just friends. I didn't either, but I don't care what I believe. I will believe whatever I have to believe to be closer to you.

I try to imagine where you were when you wrote the poem, "When I am among the trees." I feel these lyrics from the song, "You're everywhere I go, you're everything I see, I can feel that you're here tonight." I imagine I am with you in spirit everywhere you go, that I in everything you see, that I am among the trees with you, as you are with me. But oh, how I long to be one of those trees with you in the flesh. To have your arms wrapped around me.

> How kind you are to hug a tree
> > To love a bird, to love me
> How kind you are to bloom like a flower
> > To give life to children
> > To rise at your early hour
>
> How kind you are to change with the seasons
> > To keep them company
> > To grow cold in winter
> > And in spring, grow into a Garden of Eden
>
> How kind you are to be a daughter of nature
> > Loving your mother
> > Pouring yourself out as water

You are a mother, a daughter, a lover, and a friend of women. In every way, you are a woman.

-A man

3/9/2022

My Love,

Hello! How are you today? I'm good, thanks for asking! Lol.

My mood has improved a lot since yesterday. I know I told you
Kristen and I would divorce, but last time she agreed to it, she
wasn't happy about it. Yesterday she agreed, and I think she was
even a little glad to. It makes a big difference to me that she is
happy to do it, as we will have to interact for the rest of our lives,
either way.

I read your card with the story about you sitting on the lakeshore
with your eyes closed. I imagine you there again in the summer
connecting with me on the water under the heat of the sun. Your
hair is now beyond your shoulders; its length is a testament to
your promise that your hair would be long the next time I saw
you. A gentle breeze blows those long strands across your face.
Your eyes are closed as you feel my arms wrap around you. Your
hands are on your knees, and a faint smile grows across your lips.
Your skin, kissed by the sun, blushes as your heart fills with your
love for me and mine for you.

I will be there with you soon. Breathe out your worries and
breathe deeply in all of my love.

-Your Love

3/9/2022

Barbara,

I started listening to an audiobook about Buddhist psychology,
The Misleading Mind. You didn't tell me which book you were
reading. I want to know your heart so much. I'll just have to read
every book about Buddhism and psychology. I also started to
meditate. I think you are ahead of me on this, and I don't want to
get behind too far.

There are some things I said to you that I'm sorry about. When I
said, "You and David were drowning in a sea of sorrow you had
made for yourselves," I felt it was cruel to say, and I'm sorry.

My biggest fear in diving into these Buddhist ways of thinking is
that I will somehow learn to be happy without you. Well, that I
am fine with, I guess. Or I will learn to let go of you, move on,
and forget you. I am afraid of this. I am also afraid of what that
fear may be causing me to do. I will not be able to eliminate my
fears; I can only have the courage to face them, and so as I learn
more, I will hold on to the hope that I will not lose my love for
you but will try to accept it is a possibility.

The more I learn, the more I feel the stress leaving my body, and
so far, I don't feel further away or closer to you. I just feel a sense
of calmness and presence with you. It is a kind of passionless
serenity. A Yin for your Yang, if you will. I sense my spirit is
balanced by yours and yours by mine. Like a tree in a silent
garden surrounded by stones, we are together, silent and still but
very much alive.

-Mike

Barbara,

Good morning again. I don't have something specific on my mind, so I will just write whatever comes. It's a nice day today. I imagine you are appreciating it as much as I am. I have been thinking about adding something weekly to my routine. A visit to the bench of patience every Friday. Not sure why. Maybe it will symbolize that I am waiting for you. I don't know if I should be waiting for anything, even you. Maybe it will mean just that I remember you and am still in love with you. Maybe it would mean that I can't let you go, and I have some kind of attachment problem. I don't know, but I am sure I will think about you when I am there, and I am sure I will enjoy the view.

I like how you signed your 2/8 letter as "Barbara." It tells me that while you are so many things, you are the person the world knows as Barbara, the person, that same person who loves me. It tells me you are not ashamed of your love for me. Maybe you feel ashamed of your relationship or want it to be private or a secret. Sometimes I don't care what others would say one way or another. Other times I want to get on a rooftop and tell the world how much I love you. I don't think I ever felt shame about it, though sometimes I knew it wasn't the right time to mention it.

I told my family I was polyamorous about a week ago. I told my father I was when he visited me on Christmas. My father, of course, told me how sinful I was. Lisa was very open-minded and kind about it. She asked if, "There was someone I wanted to introduce her to." And I responded, "No, but thanks for asking." Elena was kind but didn't accept it. She is going through an affair Greg had. I read that 13% of marriages survive infidelity. About half break off the relationship immediately, and the rest end the marriage over time. Jessica and my mother, on the other hand, didn't respond. It feels sadly ironic of the three women I love, none of them I can kiss. This thought weighs heavily on my heart.

I'm sorry if these letters feel like a random collection of thoughts. Maybe I shouldn't tell you everything, so I have something to tell you when I see you again. Well, actually, I would love to just listen to you talk for hours and hours. The sound of your voice would run like a gentle stream on a warm day.

I don't know if you can tell yet, but I am happy right now. The card you gave me with those paintings said, "I hope sunlight and joy are finding their way to your heart." Well, they have, and you are the sunlight and joy in my heart, and they have been sent as messengers to tell me you are on the way and will be here soon.

I love you so much and can't wait to see you again.

-Mike

3/10/2022

Barbara,

I feel a presence with you right now. As I go throughout my day,
images of life with you flash into my mind; they feel so random.
As we walk up some narrow spiraling cement stairs, you're
holding my arm. The stairs are brick, red brick, and the walls are
some kind of white cement. We're very old and laughing about
something. I'm starting to let go, or I have been letting go of
conventional thinking. Maybe I just have a really active
imagination, or I'm crazy, but maybe I am connecting to a more
profound source, like the source I felt connected to when I was
with you; this is just one of the images. I thought Buddhism was
supposed to make me more present, but it seems to be taking me
somewhere else. I don't feel like I'm somewhere else. I feel
present like my consciousness is transporting me to somewhere
else, and I am with you in that sense of presence. If I really have
lived eight hundred lives with you, I have many lifetimes of being
with you. I can possibly connect to it in this way. I will continue
to explore this and keep you updated.

With love,
-Mike

Babe,

It's Friday! You know I am just taking things one day at a time, trying to get to the end of the week. Oh, I really wanted to go to our garden, but it's freezing, wet and windy. My house makes kind of a whistling sound when the wind blows, so there is a lot of whistling right now.

Today was a little more challenging; I mean, this morning, I believe Kristen is procrastinating on signing the divorce papers because she really doesn't want a divorce. There are these moments she has where I am absolutely convinced she wants the same thing as me, but then later, I realize she didn't want it at all. I'm trying to use the techniques I am learning in the audiobook I listen to to view struggle as training of the mind. I definitely feel like I feel better when I come across some difficulty throughout the day. I sat at a red light for about ten minutes this morning when dropping Daniella off. I let the frustration exist in my mind like a grey cloud. Then I just watched the cloud until the wind pushed it away.

Yesterday, I was setting some boundaries for Kristen. My therapist said I needed to do this. I told her I didn't want her to talk to my friends about me, and she said I was being controlling. I got very upset and said some very unkind things to her. The cloud was a hailstorm and did not blow away. Lol. I apologized. Today, I asked her to sign the papers, and she gave a non-affirmative response like, "I hope you have a great day" or something like that. I got super angry and responded with some angry threats, but I immediately deleted them before she read them this time. The cloud was a rainstorm. So, I was proud of myself for making some progress. The more I learn, the more I feel so much like a child. I want to have that sense of love for Kristen like I have with Daniella, but it's just not there. I see Kristen as my teacher of forgiveness now, and I think I am learning but oh, how I long for a teacher of rest, how I long for a teacher of trust and safety.

Something wonderful did happen yesterday just before I forgave her. I realized that Kristen is my teacher of forgiveness. In that moment, an overwhelming sense of peace and joy filled my heart to the point where I just started laughing. I laughed at how the pain did so well to teach me and train me. It was just very funny, and I understood that laughter to be Buddha laughter. I haven't learned about this. I only heard about it but experiencing it is not the same as learning about it. I imagine us laughing together at all the pain and the training Kristen and David will give us.

Oh, joy! How I laugh now! Lol!

-Mike

Darling,

Oh, how wise you are. I see the wisdom in everything you have done and said with each passing day. I feel so much as a child, and you see with the wisdom and love of angels. In looking back on my reactions now, I see embarrassment. I feel weak in the presence and strength of your love. I hope you will give me a chance to learn from you one day. When we first started talking, I honestly didn't know how much I could learn from you, and now, it seems there is so much more about you that I am still comprehending, and it just blows me away. What a hidden gem you are. How lucky I feel to have been able to witness the beauty of your soul.

I know also I have something to teach you. You are there when I think about my future, and I only see you when I see my future. These words give me pause, and I'm still trying to understand what they mean. I think I will know soon, but it is much more relevant to my future in this life than I originally expected.

When I say to myself, "I am polyamorous," I know it means I do love and can love more than one person at a time, but what does that really mean for my future? I had hoped for something that would include you and Kristen, and I believe that, in some way, it will. I just don't know exactly how. Does it mean you will be with me every day or just some days? Does it mean you will be in my heart only but not with me in person? I don't know, but all I see right now is you. You're the only person I see.

I will think more about this and what it means.

-Mike

3/11/2022

Barbara,

Today is a day of a lot of letters. I have a lot on my mind, I suppose.

Kristen did not sign the divorce paperwork. So, I have hired an attorney. I get the impression things are about to get quite complicated. There is so much information I have to provide for discovery. Maybe I'm just feeling overwhelmed, but may be practically, it's not that much harder than building software. Upon talking to the attorney, I definitely think it's best that we stop talking to each other. Our relationship complicates Kristen and I's divorce. And it definitely complicates or would have complicated a divorce between you and David. At this point, based on the outcome of Kristen and I's relationship, I realize the only way for us to be together is for you to divorce David. I don't think he will ever be able to accept us being together.

Another funny thing happened today. I talked to my therapist, and I told her that one of the most difficult aspects of separating from Kristen is the fact that my life will become sexless. She actually suggested that I could hire a sex worker. Lol. Not that I think there's anything wrong with that, it's just not for me, and she is basically suggesting engaging in illegal activity. Very funny, I thought. I don't know if she realizes that would complicate the divorce, or maybe she asked me that so I would hear myself saying it's a bad idea. Hmm... she's pretty good if it was the latter.

-Your Mike

3/12/2022

Barbara,

I woke up this morning and immediately began to cry. The
weight of being alone fell on my heart. Anthony and I were up all
night last night drinking. I was drinking vodka and orange juice. I
like to drink vodka more now because it reminds me of you. I
told Kristen I didn't want to be alone, so she let me go over to
her house. I thought that was nice of her. She dyed her hair black;
I've been asking her to do that for years. She told me she didn't
like it, and she also said she would cut her hair, and I wouldn't
like it. She said she would sign the divorce papers because I told
her that the discovery she would have to do would be much more
work. She tells me if I divorce, we won't be friends and that it will
be final, and she will never come back to me. She is begging me
not to file. She is calling it the "final betrayal." Honestly, it is very
hard for me, but she just isn't someone right now that I want in
my life, and there is no indication that she will start being nice to
me or start making unselfish decisions. I think there will be a lot
of stigma in her social circles. I don't understand why else she
would want to stay married to someone she mistreats. Someone
she wasn't willing to dye her hair for. I told her that we could file
a motion to dismiss the divorce proceedings if I changed my
mind after the divorce. I'm not trying to give her false hope. I'm
just looking for a way to compromise. I told her I was
uncomfortable with the combination of us being married, us not
having a sexual relationship, and her having a sexual relationship
with someone else, and that one variable needed to change. Her
first thought was to get divorced, but now that we are doing
exactly that, she asks me, "If I break things off with Jeff, will you
not file for divorce?" I told her, "No," because I did not want to
be the reason she made that decision because I thought it would
taint our relationship. Plus, I'm happy she has someone.
Unfortunately, it seems her relationship with Jeff is complicating
her decision to divorce, and I see the wisdom of breaking things
off during this period. I'm glad I don't have this kind of
complication with you. Sorry, this letter has so much about
Kristen and me. You, or rather this paper, are my confidant. This
piece of paper will understand me, I suppose. It is times like these
you realize the value of friends, even the imperfect ones and ones
that might be holding you back.

I looked up "professional cuddlers," like my therapist suggested. It's very interesting that you can pay someone to just be next to you. I think lack of physical touch is a form of suffering that can be overcome.

I was listening to the audiobook, *The Misleading Mind,* and I got to the part about how love transforms your heart, and it reminded me of your letter on February 8th, where you told me, "Your love has transformed my heart." This part also discussed the fallacy of thinking that only one person could make you happy. It also tells a story of a man who waited thirty-five years to marry his soulmate, only to divorce a year later. I will be curious if I ever do learn if this is the same book you were reading on the 8th. I understand that you will not be the same person I knew in November or December. I know that my picture of you is "frozen in time" because I cannot see how you are changing. I hope you keep sending letters so I can learn how you are changing. Even if we are ultimately never together again, I hope these letters will help offer an explanation as to how my heart is changing.

I give no promises about the future, but today, right now, I know my heart loves your heart. I am sending love and light to you.

-Mike

3/13/2022

Barb Baby,

This morning, there was a lot of love and light in my heart.

I step closer to the present as I study Buddhism. I am giving up my desires to see if doing so adds or subtracts suffering from my life. I am giving up my desire for you. I replace it with communion with your love. Oh, how liberating this is. How your love surrounds me and fills every cell in my body. How your love awakens every forgotten neuron in my brain. How your love multiplies and grows in the garden of my heart. My soul dances like a flock of birds in the sky, flying, shifting, and changing shape. I watch the wonder of your love give life and let it radiate through my skin.

I do not desire you any more than a fish desires water to swim. I swim in your love.

With Love
-Mike

Barbara, My Teacher,

I have opened the door and stepped into a new place in my mind. Because of your February 8th letter and the commitment you made to continue awakening your mind, I have found peace and joy in my heart, a garden that has been there all along. Your presence is with me everywhere I go, so I do not miss you.

I practice meditation multiple times throughout the day. I still have strong emotions, but I feel that with meditation, I am learning to bring myself back to the present when the emotion goes further than I want it to go. If I want to let the emotion bring me to tears, I can allow it, but I can stop it if I do not want it to do that. The same seems to be true about laughter, feeling offended, etc.

You have led me to the awakening of my mind, and I am grateful to you for this. Of course, I have some work to do. My ability to concentrate is improving each day.

I believe Kristen is now experiencing many similar emotions that David was. I believe she may now have a repentant heart, but that heart is full of so much fear of divorce. At first, this caught me off guard and caused some doubt about my decision, but then I catalogued the reasons for divorcing her. Then something quite wonderful happened; I was able to understand that her emotions toward me are a mixture of love and fear, and I was able to, in meditation, receive her love without receiving her fear. It's as if I constructed a spiritual forcefield around me that filtered her energy. In this way, her love brightened my heart, and I sent my love back to her. I felt confident again in my decision to divorce. I feel, also, I know how to support her even while I exercise my will for my life.

I proposed that we should get a massage together today and she accepted my invitation. Of course, I think it helped her. I started to take Monday off to give myself some extra time to reflect. It also gives me the time to prepare all the documents the lawyer requested from me.

I feel your presence so strongly with me right now. I feel the future-you that will read these letters with me. I can very nearly see you with my actual eyes. It's quite amazing what our minds are capable of. ☺

Ok, time to go.

-Mike

3/15/2022

Barbara,

The most remarkable things are happening to me. I have just made the most profound discovery about myself. I've been having difficulty concentrating for months now. So I decided to meditate on this. I have done this before, but I didn't have success. This time, I took the following strategy: I let the emotions that were distracting me form in my mind. I did not chase them away, but instead, I just let them take form and be present with my consciousness. I was not afraid of them, and once they were not afraid of me, I invited them to come with me on a walk. I walked with them and allowed them to reveal themselves to me. I got to know them. At first, I understood them to be "fear of not enough time" and "fear of lack of concentration." But then, as I stayed with these dark clouds, they became children. These children, it seemed, were alone. So, I comforted them and held them in my arms. Upon feeling my love for them, the dark clouds covering them evaporated, and I just saw children glowing with light. They were happy, and I saw them as a part of me. And I knew who they were. They were "The Ambitious One" and "The Diligent One." They were distinct. They played together. In that moment, I realized these were aspects of myself. The Ambitious One tries to do too much and is frequently afraid of not having enough time. When he is comforted, he is productive and happy. He also needs my guidance because he is a child. So I help him not try too much. The Diligent One, on the other hand, has been neglected for months. Every time he tries to work, another kid grabs my attention. So, he is sad because he cannot be diligent. He feels neglected. I comfort him by apologizing and promising to spend time with him. But when I tried, all the other children started coming to me; this is when I saw all the aspects of me or at least most of them. These are the children I saw, 20 in total:

1. The kisser:
   He likes physical affection. He is one of a group of friends that form the sexual nature in me.
2. The Writer:
   He writes poems, letters, and programming code.
3. The Activist:
   He wants things to be fair and makes a point of getting involved when things are not fair.

4.   The Companion:
     He likes to do things with his friends and feels lonely
     when he doesn't spend time with people.
5.   The Ambitious One:
     You met him already. He rallies his friends to accomplish
     difficult tasks.
6.   The Thinker:
     This one is also a problem solver. He plays a lot with the
     planner and the writer.
7.   The Diligent One:
     He can work for long hours without stopping. He is best
     friends with The Ambitious One and The Planner. Also,
     he is inseparable from The Thinker.
8.   The Dreamer:
     This one thinks big and imagines all types of wonderful
     things. He is the inspiration for The Ambitious One, The
     Diligent One, The Romantic, The Writer, and so many
     other kids.
9.   The Romantic:
     He can always be seen carrying a rose and daydreaming.
10. The Organizer:
     This one loves to clean and tidy up. He hangs out a lot
     with the planner and the thinker.
11. The Relaxer:
     This one pretty much hangs out by himself. Sometimes
     though, he shares a conversation with The Artist.
12. The Planner:
     He has a plan for literally everything. He can easily get
     carried away if he spends too much time with the
     perfectionist.
13. The Explorer:
     Also, he could be called "The Learner" and is insatiably
     curious.
14. The Listener:
     He doesn't say much, but everyone wants to have a
     conversation with him.
15. The Artist:
     He has a very geometric art style most of the time. He
     sometimes will do drawings for The Thinker and The
     Planner.
16. The Creator / Destroyer:
     This one is the most admired and feared by the other
     children. Only the dreamer is not afraid of him. They
     work and play really well together. The Creator is the one

that can pull together the dreamers' big ideas and make them a reality. He has no problem destroying anything between him and the accomplishment of his project. He is the Phoenix.

17. The Showoff:
This one loves to be admired. He takes all the credit for what the other kids make. He likes to dress up and persuades The Diligent One and The Ambitious One to go to the gym with him.

18. The Sensitive One:
Constantly getting paper cuts, this kid is super bipolar. He can go from super happy to super sad in an instant. He requires a lot of attention to keep him from getting out of control, and his best friend is The Romantic.

19. The Thrill-Seeker
He is an adrenaline junkie and loves to hang out with The Explorer and The Kisser. These three make up my sexual nature. Recently, he started hanging out with The Romantic.

20. The Perfectionist:
Loves to throw a pity party with the sensitive one when someone criticizes them for a mistake. He cleans, programs, and is just rude sometimes.

I may discover other children, but I think I have my hands full for now. To me, the model of children is more useful than clouds because it seeks to accept our aspects and does so with tender love rather than only ignoring or just dismissing them when they are not happy.

I will get to know these children more, and as I do and learn to take care of them, I believe I will create a house of joy and laughter within me.

-Mike

3/16/2022

Barbara,

I made a plan for the day that gives me only 12 more minutes to write this letter. I have been thinking that putting these letters in envelopes won't be very convenient for you and that when you're old, you would prefer to have something like a book to hold instead.

I have read your February 8th letter so many times, and there is something pivotal for us in that letter. I dissect it into these sections:

- We see each other. We are seen by each other.
- We will not be apart forever. Hope for our relationship.
- We need a different path to reach each other.
- You need time to grow, and so do I.
- We love each other. Our love is timeless.

It was a call to action for me, and I am taking it. I am here with you, my love. Be with yourself. When the tidal waves try to drown you, remember you can breathe under water.

-Mike

Barbara,

Today, I am writing you a letter in a notebook instead of putting it in an envelope.

Yesterday, I was complaining to my brother about Kristen. He pointed out that my energy may affect Daniella's attitude towards her. Daniella is very upset with Kristen, and I think she blames her for me moving out and not being able to see you. If she does have a telepathic link, then Anthony is right. So today, I focused on forgiving her during my meditation. I imagined that Kristen and I were standing outside a burnt-down house in my meditation. Kristen is a child. She started the fire that burnt down the house, and she was very sad about it. I also am partially responsible because I left the matches out. We both stand there looking at the house. Daniella is also there with us. She says, "That's ok, we can get a new house." A huge smile grows in me as I say, "Yes, we can, and we will." I try to hug Kristen to comfort her, but she is overwhelmed with guilt. So, I imagine holding her in my imagination. I give all of my love to her. She says, "We can fix it." I responded with a gracious smile, "No, we cannot fix it, but that's ok." She sobs and lets me hold her now. Trying to cheer her up, I tell her we will have a lot of fun while looking for a new house. We can sleep in a tent and under the stars in a treehouse. We can stay with our friends. I tell her, "We learned a lot about what we like and don't like about houses." Now when we find a new house, we can get one that has all the things we like and without all the things we don't like." She asks, "Will we live together?" I replied, "I don't think so, but you can sometimes stay over at my place if you like." She nods with a sad but accepting posture. I then take her by the hand towards the playground.

I will continue to focus on this feeling of forgiveness and optimism about the new houses we will live in. The house is our relationship. I know she will want to fix the burnt-down house, and I will be gracious when she does, but I will not try to help her. I will be patient and understanding, and if she wants, I will go to the playground with her.

I think about the words at the end of your letter. You use the word "desire." According to the Buddhist philosophy, desire leads to suffering. At first, this was confusing to me. How can we have goals then if we have no desires? I understand now that we do not need goals any more than the tiger needs a goal to eat a deer. A tiger just is a tiger. We should just be what we are rather than try to achieve goals. If we are a goat, then we will climb mountains. Rather than try to grow fruit on a tree, we can just simply take fruit from another tree. We do not need to fix a burnt-down house. We can just find a new house. Trying to fix it, blaming, and crying about it won't bring the house back. We also don't need to look for a house. We will find one while we are enjoying the adventure of being homeless.

Enjoy this beautiful day with me. Talk to you soon.

-Mike

Barb Babe,

I hope you're well and hope the sunlight is finding its way into your heart. I am struggling with expressing myself right now because I am trying to let go of my desires. So, the words "hope," "wish," and "want" all express desire, and I must admit that I have not completely given up my desires. Why am I trying to do this? Well, the more I learn about Buddhism, the more I learn that desire causes suffering, and in practicing giving up desire, I experience less suffering. It is hard to say how far I can or will go with this, but I am experiencing a wave of inner peace and happiness in my life. Maybe some of this is caused or influenced by the mood stabilizer I am taking, and maybe some is caused by the meditation. I feel so much more grounded. I feel I am growing roots into the ground! My meditation takes me to such deep states of confidence and emotional stability like I have never before experienced in my life, and this is all because of your letter and the intention for me you showed in writing it.

Your words in your letter, "My desire now is to gain the strength to express myself." I hope this desire does not cause you suffering. Perhaps like me, it's difficult to separate intent from desire. I believe you already have this strength inside you. You just need to find it.

I will say with the only words I have now; I wish you could see all the light, love, and peace in me.

I do not feel closer to you, meaning there is still so much I do not know about you, but I feel your presence more than I ever have. When I meditate, you are in the same room of light with me. You are not millions of light-years apart. You radiate peace and joy in white and violet. We are the only ones in this room, and we are happy.

I love you now. Right now, I love you. Read that as often as you want, and it will be true.

-Mike

Barbara,

Today's meditation was intense. Towards the end, I could feel the blood moving throughout my body. My heart was shaking my body subtly but noticeably. I could hear the blood rushing in my head with each pump of my heart. I could speed up and slow down my heart rate. Amazingly, I could feel the individual hairs on my skin like trees swaying in the wind.

Desires and ideas flew by and landed next to me like birds. As I led them, we all sat together, breathing in while saying "one" and breathing out while saying "two." I did not reject, dismiss, or ignore them, but I asked them to join me. I accepted them.

My eyes saw indescribable wonders between each breath I drew in and each one I let out—a lot of clouds, cities founded long ago, the statue of Buddha, a host of seaweed springing to life as I glided across the ocean floor, a shoreline of the ocean, portals from space to the clouds on earth, and a lot of other things I can't explain or remember. The clouds always move like expanding fractals and in an accelerated way like time was passing faster than it does while I am awake. All of this brings me to the question, "What really are we?" Surely, "human" is insufficient if we can easily see these visions.

I just noticed my handwriting was a little hard to read. Sorry.

Time does seem to be passing faster, which I like because that means you'll be in my arms sooner. Is that a desire? I wonder. I will meditate on it.

You once asked if I would fall in love with you again. Honestly, I haven't fallen out of love with you. I had a vision last night while meditating. You told me I would fall asleep next to you very soon every night. I think this would be a good thing. Whether falling asleep or falling in love, I know I will enjoy it if I am doing it with you.

-Mike

Barb,

I had a thought. I thought that the purpose of the suffering we have endured in our marriages was so we could appreciate each other. I don't think I could have appreciated Kristen if I did not experience Stacy, and I think the same thing is true about you. There must be suffering to understand joy. There must be darkness to understand light. There must be a Yin to understand Yang.

It's funny now that when I see darkness in my life or the world, I also see the light, and the darker the darkness is, the brighter the light shines.

Oh, how bright you shine in my heart!

-Mike

Barb,

I have finished another meditation, and I realized that the images of the sky and under water I saw during my meditation are from other lives I lived as a bird. Some kind of bird that can go under water briefly. Maybe a bald eagle or maybe something more pre-historic like a tetradactyl. I saw little baby birds, too. I was looking down on them, feeding them; this made me smile. They were my children.

I don't know if most people have these kinds of visions when meditating, but I find it absolutely fascinating.

I feel like I am starting to see people differently. I feel like you wrote in your letter: "To see others as they truly are." If I am a being that was a bird and is now a person who has lived many lives and spent time in between, then other people are likely something similar. It's easier not to look at a single instance of someone's behavior and think, "This is all that this person is." Like "they are rude" or "they are kind." It's easier to look at someone's behavior and ask instead, "What aspect of this being are you?" "Are you remembering your life as a fish and fear my energy as a bird?" "Are you remembering your life as a tiger or a hungry deer?"

"What really are you?"

No matter how often we ask this question, we may never know the answer. So far, I can find that regardless of what someone is doing, I am more often to have an attitude of curiosity. When they help me answer the question by continuing a particular behavior, I accept what they are.

I expect I have not asked this question nearly enough times of you to hear the answer, nor have I observed you often enough to accept the answer, but I expect that I will.

-Mike

Barbara,

I am making a transition from a goal-oriented intention to a self-alignment-oriented intention. Sometimes this is easy, and sometimes it is difficult because I do not have this as muscle memory. I am listening to an audiobook, *Buddha's Brain*. It is about the neuroscience of Buddhism, and I think you may like it or at least be able to explain the concepts to me. There was a quote that read, "I feel that I am in the process of physically rewiring my brain." Doing something to achieve something is how my brain currently works. Doing something because that is who I am is a new reason to do something. Sometimes when I think about why I am doing something, the phrase "Everything I do, I do for you" comes to mind. This will not work, though I believe there is some connection. When I look at your picture, I see myself in you more each time. When I meditate, you are frequently with me. The word "you" starts to gain dual ownership of meaning for Barbara and me; this happens so frequently that the line between Mike and Barbara in the word "you" gets blurred so that, in some cases, I can't tell who I actually mean when I have a thought with the word "you." So, when I think, "Everything I do, I do for you," who is "you?" Is it me, or is it Barbara, or is it us? I think about how my inner being has multiple aspects, and all these aspects come together to live with my consciousness. I wonder now if an inner being can have multiple parts and live inside one living thing, can an inner being have multiple parts and live inside two living things? Are you and I part of the same inner being living inside two separate bodies? Can we join our consciousness into one consciousness, or is it already partially joined? I will think and meditate on this more, but I can tell you with absolute certainty that the connection I feel with you is orders of magnitude large and stronger than anything I have ever felt with anyone else in my entire life. I just do not believe there is someone comparable in existence. Maybe I'm wrong; I guess I'll only know when I'm on my death bed. Anyways, what I was getting to was when I think about the reason I do something, it feels more accurate to me now to say, "We do this because this is who we are." Almost as if there is no separate concept in harmony with just "I" in my understanding of what I am. Maybe this is similar to thinking of a single leg. It can only be in harmony when it is in the context of both legs, especially if you're trying to get somewhere. I guess what I am saying is I feel like we are part of the same entity or being, and getting anywhere without one another is like someone hopping on one foot. Lol. Funny.

Do you get what I'm saying yet? ☺

-Mike

3/21/2022

Barbara,

I will tell you again how my meditation is evolving. I meditate for about thirty minutes three times a day now. It is so powerful that I can overcome personal issues in just a few meditation sessions rather than weeks or years. It's allowing me to access my subconscious like ecstasy but without the negative side effects. Yesterday, I did a meditation where all my aspects came out of my body, and yours came out too, and they were like stars circling a galaxy, blue and yellow, white, and violet, just circling together in between us. I mean, between our bodies. As I have been getting into these meditative states, waves of goosebumps continuously roll across my skin; it is very real. When I open my eyes, I do not immediately have control of my motor functions. So I have to start by wiggling my fingers.

Have you experienced anything like this?

-Mike

3/21/2022

Barbara,

I will wait for you, but I will be happy while waiting.

-Mike

3/22/2022

Barbara,

This morning, I woke up late and didn't have time to meditate before Daniella went to school, so I was practicing being present and focusing on what I was doing instead of letting my mind wander like it usually does. I found I was more engaged, cheerful, and playful. Some people might laugh at my realization that I will be more engaged if I am present, but I just didn't experience the effect of intentionally being present. Children seem to respond very well to this shift. I have been noticing how people interact with me is changing. Very unintentionally, people seem to be more drawn to me. There is an outward effect of what is happening to me; this is very similar to falling in love. You once told me, "[You're] glad [you] were wearing a mask because you cannot hide your smile." This happiness is not the same, not as strong as that, but it seems more consistent, like contentment or deep satisfaction rather than excitement. And Barbara, I feel this way all day long!

I thought about how divorce can feel like a non-acceptance of my present, but I feel that it is not a contradiction. If the wind blows on my face or my back, it will not affect the direction I am walking. If the wind is a hurricane, I might take shelter until it has passed, but I will continue in the same direction. I feel the wind, like my emotions, but I do not follow them every time they change direction.

I see you staying with David as taking shelter in a hurricane. The sun will shine again, and you will continue your journey.

To me, continuing on the path, our destiny, to become the truest version of ourselves regardless of the pain it causes ourselves and others, is like drawing our attention back to our breath. When we cry, or someone else cries, we do not fight the experience or run away with it. We acknowledge it, love it, accept it, and ask it to be with us. Just like when we meditate, we do not fight our thoughts and emotions. Instead, we acknowledge them, love them, accept them, and ask them to sit with us as we return our attention to our breath and keep breathing. People may get very upset when we show clarity and resolve in our life, especially if they were used to being able to shift our perspective on what we are and the path of our life, but that is just someone we love and accept as we continue walking.

Keep walking your path, and I will see you when you get to where we are going, "the rendezvous point."

-Mike

Barb Babe,

Good morning, Oi. I need to make some coffee! Ok, I'm back.

There is a huge smile floating across my heart. Yesterday, we celebrated Kristen getting a job offer as a front-end developer. And she told me that you emailed her. To know that you were somewhere, wearing clothes, pressing your fingers down on a keyboard, looking at a computer screen gives me so much joy. It is the only thing I know about what you are doing with your life, and I am so grateful to have learned this one thing about you.

Yesterday, I decided that if I don't see you before December 3rd, I will publish these letters with names changed and my identity hidden and send you a copy. Hey, maybe I should do that anyway ☺.

I listened to the song O by Coldplay a few times. Obviously, the piano reminds me of you, but the lyrics really made me think of us.

> A flock of birds
> Hovering above
> Just a flock of birds
> That's how you think of love

You have such a deep connection with nature, and I sometimes wonder if you think about our love as something that happened or something that is. I am hovering above but not like a flock of birds; I hover like a griffin with golden armored feathers.

-Mike

3/23/2022

Barbara,

The more I meditate on your choices, the more awe of their
wisdom I see. I mean, you have made such wise choices despite
the pain they caused to everyone. I have so much admiration for
you.

I realized today that this time of us not talking is important for
Kristen, so she does not feel like you took me away from her. I
don't want her to be bitter towards you, and this is really the only
way. It does cause me great pain, but there is a purpose to the
pain, and this pain is causing me to grow in ways I could have
only ever dreamed of.

The same concept applies to David, too, I think. He needs to see
that he is not competing with me. I think it's also helping us be
more confident that our marriages are not helping us become the
best versions of ourselves regardless of what you and I have. I
think there is quite a number of months ahead before everyone
fully accepts that the old relationships are over and can move on,
but I do believe we are moving in that direction, thanks to you.

-Mike

3/24/2022

Barbara,

Yesterday evening was such a strong experience for me. I was
meditating before bed, and Daniella asked if she could come into
my room. I normally do not let her in my room because I have
some adult paintings on the wall. So, I took down the paintings
and let her come in. As I was meditating, she crawled into my lap
and told me, "Papa, I love you one million thousand." I dotingly
told her, "I love you one million thousand too." Then she said,
"Papa, I do not want you to die." I told her it would be a very
long time before I'd die, so we don't have to worry about that
right now. She asked, "How long?" I answered, "Like sixty
years," then asked, "Can you count to sixty?" She responded
immediately, "No! I do not want to count to sixty!" I said, "Ok, it
will be about twenty thousand days." She then slowly said, "Ok,
that is a lot of days. But can you try not to die? Because I do not
know how to live without you. Can you try to live one million
days?" I told her, "I will try to live one million days."

I couldn't write this without two tissues. Barbara, I am sharing
this beauty in my life only to you.

I am trying to give up things in my life, like desire and control.
Last night before that conversation, I was meditating on an
emotion running away with me a little. That's why I knew I
needed to meditate on it. I was feeling the separation from you. I
believe some part of me still desires you to be with me, which
causes me suffering, so I try to let go of this desire. I feel better
now. It is a fine line to walk between not desiring your soulmate,
the woman you love and waiting patiently for her. I know that
walking this path of pain and uncertainty is my path, and I will do
it every day, all twenty thousand of them because I love you a
million thousand.

Mike
&
Barbara

-Mike

Barbara,

I have begun to develop a new theory about the children inside
of me. It actually became easier to see after I discovered a new
child in me, "The Accountant," which now makes 21 children.
Buddhists teach that attachments cause suffering. What if these
children are not only aspects of myself but also attachments that I
have? There was a quote I also came across that I can't find now
but said something to the effect of "do not hold on to the image
of yourself." I understood that to mean that if we let go of our
identity, we can truly experience everything as it actually is rather
than through the lens of our opinions and experiences. Maybe if
we help these children grow up just by loving them and taking
care of them, we can let go of the attachments they form. One
might have to become a monk to let go of all attachments. Don't
worry; I can't do this while I have a daughter who is still a child.

I have decided today that you are my teacher of patience, and
Kristen is my teacher of restraint. Lol. Thanks, teachers!

-Mike

Barb,

I'm sitting at my desk again. Thankfully, my collar bone is getting a little better each day. It's easier to write when you can rest one arm on the desk, and I couldn't do that.

It's about 5 a.m. now. I have been meditating for the last five hours. I went to sleep around 9 p.m and awoke around 12 a.m. Kristen sent me a text saying that "there was no point in talking to me since I did what I wanted to do anyway." In other words, she cannot manipulate me anymore. We were trying to find a solution to temporarily address Daniella's issues at school. For the last three Wednesdays, she has gotten into trouble. She stays with Kristen on Tuesdays. So I offered to switch Sunday and Tuesday until we can figure out what is going on. We have a play therapy session scheduled in a couple of weeks. Kristen wanted to add Wednesday and wouldn't have it any other way, so I just told her we'd keep things the same and went to bed. I was very disturbed by her message because instead of arguing, I just decided to accept things as they are and risk Daniella potentially getting kicked out of school. And I was being accused of doing whatever I wanted. So, I meditated on this for about two hours without any success. Then I had a panic attack. Again, I meditated for another couple of hours. What got me through it was letting go of two children/attachments: the Accountant (money) and The Companion (friendship). I have had a great deal of anxiety that Kristen will try to get alimony from me in the divorce, so I am filled with this fear every time she is unhappy with me. I let go of this attachment by ensuring the accountant that he was grown up enough to go on by himself and that everything would be in balance no matter what happened. I appreciate everything he has done for me—the same thing with the companion.

I feel quite happy again. I don't need any particular friend because I am already part of a community of life. I don't really need money because it's just part of life and many or most living things live without it. It does feel quite interesting to me to not have these attachments to friends or money. These things have been so essential and desired by me my whole life. Hope this story helps you with any attachments you still have.

-Mike

3/25/2022

Barbara,

I must admit right now that I miss you. I don't know if it's the
kind of missing that wishes you were here or the kind that simply
cherishes the thought of your presence, but I feel it to be more of
the latter.

It is Friday night now. I am at my house by myself. A little while
ago, I thought this was sad, but now, I find the opportunity in it.
I can do whatever I love to do. I love writing to you.

I saw you signed into Telegram today. I did have an urge to
message you but decided against it. I really want you to be
confident that your leaving David is because of what you want
for your life and not my influence.

Whenever I meditate now, you are always with me, but today,
Kristen was there also. I believe she realized or at least started to
see how much she hurt me today. I really hope the pain she feels
right now catalyzes change inside her. She has already lost me,
and she is losing Daniella too. In my meditation today, I sensed
that you and Kristen's time to re-connect and heal has started.
Maybe I am wrong about this; I think the distancing I am doing
from her may somehow encourage her to be more open to the
idea of reconnecting with you, even though this is not my intent.
I hope something good comes from this time for both of you. I
have now released you both.

Fly doves! Fly away!

-Mike

My love,

There are so many ways to love. I'm so grateful I had the opportunity to love in marriage. You know, in the U.S., only 5 in 1,000 people get married per year? It is at an all-time low. I think I got pretty lucky to get married before dating apps were invented. Apparently, dating apps are not helping to create more marriages that last forever. I don't think about divorce as a failed marriage, not because it's inappropriate but because it's not helpful. I like to think about it more like a graduation ☺. The number of graduating marriages continues to increase while the total number of marriages decreases. Women in their twenties have option overload. They use dating apps for validation, whereas before, they would go out to get the validation, and once their options decrease to a manageable level, they don't like what is left. The top 10% of men date the top 40% of women, while the top 90% of women only want to date the top 5% of men; this leaves 60% of women dating nobody and 80% of men dating nobody. Of course, just because you can date doesn't mean it will turn into love. All the more reason I am grateful I don't have to deal with all that.

I have loved in dating. I have loved in marriage. I have loved more than one woman while being married. I have loved and will keep loving as a father. I have loved as a brother and a friend. Yet there are still more ways to love. I will love as an ex-husband and maybe a grandparent and an uncle. Perhaps as a stranger, a co-worker, or a boss.I am looking forward to all the other ways to love, and it will be pleasant to enjoy those different ways of loving with you.

While meditating, I had these two thoughts, and I will share them with you.

Do not hope for love. Love for hope.

A bee does not care for the grass, but a grasshopper does

I am sending my love and light to you now.

Love,
-Mike

3/26/2022

Barbara,

I'm sitting outside right now under the stars. It's funny that I say "right now" because we are always under the stars. I notice so many things now! I remember when we were looking up at the stars at the lake house. I remember when you told me about the three stars that aligned with the moon. There is this side of you, this connection to nature that you have that I am just beginning to see and understand. See, I have found a way to get to know you even though you are not here. I started this journey with Buddhism and meditation because I wanted to be closer to you, but it seems to me the more I learn and understand, the more I realize how much further ahead you are. I see the things you said to me so differently. I see them through your heart.

I couldn't help but feel how much of life I have missed by not living in the moment. I couldn't help but cry as I looked up at the night sky and felt the gravity of the impact you have had on me. No one else even comes close. This desire is causing me suffering: I want so much to hold you right now.

-Mike

My love!

Good morning! You know my favorite part of waking up now is
that I get to write you another letter ☺. I know sometimes I write
more than one in a day, but I still feel like I still have some things
to share with you no matter how much time passes. No matter
how much I share, there is something new. When you sent me
that picture of you holding a rose, you wrote, "You are amazing.
I believe that we can keep our love fresh and romantic forever."
It seems that, at least in my heart, this is true. I imagine a life with
you where we wake up each day with one another and receive a
letter from the other person. In this picture, we are old and have
been doing this for many years ☺. I am getting better at
separating desire from accepting and cherishing a thought or idea
we would enjoy. Desire does bring suffering because we do not
have what we want, creating a kind of emptiness, a hold, or a
sense of loss. Accepting and cherishing an idea is an openness to
the possibility of something and accepting the enjoyment that
things might bring without expecting that it should or must
happen so that we do not feel disappointed when it doesn't
happen but still enjoy it if it does. I am working on doing this
more each day, and in your words, "It will take time and internal
work. And I believe that I'm capable to do this work of
liberation."

I imagine what I would be like without your Feb 8th letter. What
would I have done if you did not know those "four dark days?"
What would you have done? This reminds me of the lyrics in a
song that was really meaningful to me in the month after I moved
out, *Father Ocean (Ben Böhmer Remix)*.

> Ocean father, I was wrong
> Years I followed just the sun
> Now I see your darkness holds the key
> I close my eyes, and I begin to see

I think I would be confused, lost, and still struggling. But I think
what has been more important is that I was left to find my own
way in the darkness. You set a light up on a hill, but I still had to
get there on my own.

I wonder how Kristen will find her way. I would enjoy it very much if she did. I still love her very much and "will always do." I think it is fine to imagine a future where we both can be happy in some way. I know she wants to hurt me right now because she is afraid. I think I could eventually learn to allow myself to feel this pain without suffering, but I feel that right now, she needs to feel the pain of realizing she is hurting someone she cares about. Maybe that pain can lead her to realize she is doing it because of fear, and she'll be able to accept whatever she is afraid of. I must admit I am very much tempted to help her come to this conclusion, but I feel that she needs to find this on her own right now. I also had to overcome a fear that I had by accepting that the fear may be fulfilled.

I think there are two ways to overcome fear, but most people only rely on or mostly rely on one of them. They can be illustrated in this analogy. Let's suppose that a six-foot-four-inch three-hundred-pound man is walking toward you with a menacing look on his face, and we have a knife in our hand. Suppose we stab him pre-emptively only to find out that he was just having a bad day. We feel terrible because he is a volunteer nurse with three kids. Lol. You get the picture. Now we ask ourselves, how could we have handled that differently?

1.   We re-assure ourselves that he is just a guy walking down the street
2.   We accept that this guy may kill us

Most people rely on being reassured that fear should not be feared. E.g., "I won't take your kids from you" or "I won't sue you for alimony." The problem with this is that it relies on someone else or information we don't have. Instead, if we said, "They may take my kids from me. This will be painful, but there is a purpose to the pain, and I do not have to suffer," or "They may sue me for alimony, but money isn't everything, and happiness doesn't depend on it," we can overcome the fear all by ourselves, and no one can take that courage. We can enjoy it if the fear is not fulfilled and not become unhappy if it does. What is fear if it is not a desire for something not to happen?

I don't know when you'll read it, but maybe this could help you with a fear you are struggling with. Maybe it will help you enjoy a beautiful day like the one we have today if you are reading this on a beautiful day ;)

I love you

-Mike

3/28/2022

Barbara Baby,

I am in the process now of developing a new routine and schedule. At present, I have these things. I meditate for about 30 minutes after I wake up, during lunch, and before going to sleep. After I meditate in the morning, I write to you, and on the nights Daniella is not with me, I write to you. I just bought a stationary bike, so I can start exercising again. I haven't been able to do much of anything since I broke my clavicle. Now at least I can walk and do chores around the house like washing the dishes. I recently read a quote that I cannot find but was something to the effect of "Whatever you do, do it slowly and purposefully." I have been trying to practice this even in my letter today. Can you tell the difference in the writing? Is it easier to read? In my experience, in my startups, going faster doesn't necessarily become synonymous with getting done sooner because you burn out. One of the things I enjoy about my letters to you is I get to confess my imagination to you. I just found this quote: "What you think you become. What you feel you attract. What you imagine you create." Every time I write these letters and often when I meditate, I imagine life with you; what it might be like if we share any part of this life together.

This morning in my meditation, I was focusing on giving up attachments. These ones were top of mind:
- Attachment to attachments
- Fear I may never talk to or see you again
- Fear I may never have any kind of positive relationship with Kristen again
- Fear I may have to pay Kristen alimony for the next five years or until she marries
- Fear I may never have sex again
- Fear love may never find me again
- Attachment to following a particular plan or schedule for my life
- Attachment to Daniella
- Attachment to trying to be a good father
- Attachment to being physically attractive
- Fear of not having any friends

As I acknowledged and accepted that these fears might be fulfilled and these attachments are not needed and can be lost, a vision of me in a canoe going down a river appeared. I thought to myself, "What an interesting life it would be if all of my fears became true and I lost all of my attachments but was still happy." I sensed deep happiness in me that could not be taken by anything or person. It seems to be that deeply grounded happiness comes from applying your thoughts each day to create your imagination without having any expectations of exactly how that imagination will represent itself.

> The less we hold onto in our minds, the more we can hold onto with our hands

You are not in my arms right now, but I imagine each day that you are. In me, this imagination is consistent. I accept that this imagination may not be fulfilled in this life, but I imagine it nonetheless. I do not fight or cling to thoughts of you. I simply accept them, and they come to me every day. I make no promise that they will continue, but they have persisted every day since September 4th, the first day you wrapped your arms around me, 205 days ago, more than half a year.

I see a perfect crescent moon from my seat on the couch right now. I hear five planets align in April and 6 in June. I imagine seeing you very soon.

-Love
Mike

Barbara,

Good morning ☺. Today, I woke up early at 2:30 a.m. and was out of bed at 3:00 a.m. I focused on feeling my skin, muscles, and organs in meditation. For the second day in a row, my leg fell asleep. My current theory is that the intense focus on the other parts of my body slows my heart rate and breathing to the point that my leg doesn't get enough oxygen. So probably, I am getting too far ahead of myself, and it would be better if I just focused on my breathing for now. It's so interesting that I felt so much awareness after sleeping for only six hours.

I went for a walk yesterday, practicing gratitude and forgiveness for some people and groups of people that have caused me pain. The further down this journey I go, the more I realize how much work I can do on myself. I see how much ill-will I have been harboring in so many areas of my life. There are so many people, especially me, who need forgiveness. The more things I let go of, the stronger your presence feels. As I was walking, I could feel you next to me as if you were there. Eventually, Kristen came also. We all were peaceful and happy and had forgiven each other for everything. I tried to sense David, but he was not with us; he was far away.

When I look at objects right now, I see the energy they radiate. I see the space between their atoms; this was the experience I had when you wrote your blue and yellow poem for me. I feel the vibration of the blood rushing through my veins. It seems that I have now all the power of those moments, that sense and belief that the entire universe was designed so that you and I could love each other. I feel a sense of permanence in my existence, and your presence is a part of that. As I walk and move throughout the day, I feel you are with me so strongly that sometimes I change where I am walking so that I can avoid running into you. My sense of your presence is like a ghost I share my life with all day long.

I

    Love

        You,

            Barbara

                        -Mike

Protons,

More and more of me falls away each day and moment. My
opinions often cause me suffering, so I release them all the time.
By the time I see you again, I wonder if there will be anything left
of what I was for you to be in love with. Will there be an answer
to the question, "Who are you?" I am letting go of myself, and
that self is what you loved. Did you really love my soul or just the
clothes my soul was wearing? When you see me again, will you
recognize me? I do believe that the fear I had about Buddhism
causing me to stop loving you has not come to pass. But while I
feel like I am shifting from loving who you are to loving what you
are, I feel "I love you" holds nonetheless. It might be accurate to
say I am shifting towards a "this loves that" and redescribing the
word love to mean that it is not a choice or feeling but a state of
existing relative to one another. That is to say, I am starting to
think about our love as more of objective observation of two
things bound together. Like scandium has twenty-one electrons
and twenty-one protons, I have twenty-one aspects/children.
You are those protons. What makes the electrons form a cloud
rather than just shoot into oblivion? Should we call that force
that binds atoms together love? Those electrons are only called a
"cloud" in the context of their relationship to the protons.
Together, they make an atom, but apart, they are not anything at
all. In such a way, now, I am, and you are.

I really am sorry if there is not a "me" for you to love. I wonder
what you are now, and whatever entity is held inside that body I
held, will it love the entity which can only exist within the context
of you?

Sorry, it's a strange letter.

I mean to write that I may be less of the "I" when I see you
again. You may not love the new entity inside this body, which is
ok. If anything, I don't know what I am, and I realize that lack of
something may be difficult to love. So, to clarify, I love whatever
you are because "I" does not even exist without you.

Love,
-Electron Cloud

Barbara,

This morning I had a headache. Hence I almost decided not to
meditate, but I did. Instead of focusing on my breathing, I
focused on the pain. I have noticed when I have had back pain
while sitting upright because my muscles are not strong enough,
I accept and love the pain if I focus on it, and it becomes a part
of me. It does not scream for attention or set off alarm bells. The
pain feels less uncomfortable until the sensation that the pain
brings no longer meets the definition of pain. It is more like
carrying a moderately heavy weight where you know it is there,
but not too heavy. When I continued focusing on this pain until
that pain was the only thing in my awareness, the pain
disappeared completely. There was a purpose to this pain; it
taught me so much about handling really intense, persistent pain
that I have no control over. I could not feel pain when pain is all
I felt because pain can only exist in the context of a lack of pain,
just like light can only exist in the context of a lack of light. I
cannot write on black paper with black ink. There was no pain
within pain; there was just pain, and as soon as pain was all I
could see, pain no longer existed. I believe this is the same
phenomenon that the brain creates when we say, "To lose the
forest for the trees." We can use this aspect of our brains to our
advantage. If the forest is a forest of pain, we can focus on a tree
to lose the forest. That is to say, a forest is only considered a
forest because parts of the earth are not covered in trees. So, if
we look only at one tree, the forest doesn't exist. We lose track of
our heartbeat and breathing because they are happening all the
time. Counterintuitively, something which takes the entirety of
our focus ceases to exist.

Problems in relationships can be addressed in the same way or
created in the same way. If we were on an island and grew up
with only one other person and did not know of the existence of
any other relationships, we would be perfectly happy with that
person because, to us, the relationship wouldn't exist. It would
simply be our way of life. The only thing to compare our
interaction with them would be the time we are alone.
Unfortunately, this solution is not possible in our lives. Still, it's
possible that if we put all of our focus on one relationship that
the relationship would cease to exist, and we would be able to
then compare our interaction with them to being alone. This, I

suppose, is what you and I are doing now. When I am alone now, I am really so happy compared to when I am with Kristen. At first, it was the opposite because I was dependent on her for physical intimacy and affection. Now I don't feel a really strong need for physical touch or even sex of any kind. Without that addiction drawing me back to her, I realize there is almost nothing positive for me in the relationship right now. She cannot be a confidant even because she doesn't understand me anymore.

My meditation practices help me be nonreactive to her attempts to push my buttons, and when I don't react, she really freaks out. I still fail sometimes, though, and she gets a reaction from me, giving her the validation she is looking for. I think what I learned from today's headache will help me deal with the pain she gives me. Rather than trying to deflect or simply accept the pain, if I put all of my focus on it, eventually, it will cease to exist. This reminds me of the moment I told you on January 18th that I basically felt used by you. You said, "It hurts so much now. Do not tell anything. Please, I have to deal with my pain." I can imagine you were applying some acceptance technique or focusing on the pain to make it disappear.

So, I am close to the point you were at on January 18th. I imagine you have grown much since then, but I wonder in what ways. I will continue to try to grow so that you are not too far ahead of me. I would like it if we were a match on spiritual and emotional maturity.

I am feeling so happy and confident again. I am laughing. I am starting to get on a schedule. I sleep less because my sleep is more restful. I know I have so much work to do on myself. I would enjoy getting to know each other again, I think.

Thank you for leading me to this point. Because of you, I have found happiness within me that cannot be taken.

Love,
-A man that loves you very, very much

Barbara,

Good morning. Today we woke up a little late but somehow managed to get to school on schedule. The house is a wreck, but somehow, it doesn't bother me as much as it might have used to. It's not that I'm not interested in having a clean house; it's just that I know I have been prioritizing, and I accept the situation I find myself in as a result. I am happy because I meditate 90 minutes a day, and I wouldn't trade that happiness for a clean house because a clean house will not make me happy.

Yesterday, Daniella and I went to a play therapist. She painted some things; a mermaid, a blue sun and something she could not name. It reminded me of the painting Karen made that was a picture of how she felt. I find it very interesting to imagine how the painting will help Daniella stop school misbehaviour.

I have finished the audiobook *Buddha's Brain*. Toward the end, it discussed how losing the sense of self can help create a heightened sense of awareness and objectivity. I am still very reactive to the things Kristen says to me. I would like it if I was able to be less reactive. Placing myself in the third person seems to be helping, so rather than observing that "She said I am bad or unworthy," I can observe that "That woman said these words" or "That said this." Removing the characterizations like "good" and constructs like "woman" helps remove emotion. Removing identities such as "she" and "I" removes the single position perspective that a person has and the subjectivity from the event. This reframing helps create an objective and unbiased perspective on the event that enables me to decide which course of action or inaction will create more alignment with my true self.

I have started a new audiobook, *How to Talk so Little Kids Will Listen*, upon the recommendation of the play therapist. I can't help but think about how good you are with kids and how attractive that is to me. I think about Kristen's interactions with Daniella, and I wonder how much modeling Kristen is doing of her own mother. She didn't talk much about her mother. I only remember her telling me how her mother was frustrated that she couldn't do math. I wonder if her mother was overbearing. I don't think Kristen ever fully healed from losing her mother. Maybe it's hard for Kristen to admit she made mistakes because her mother would punish her if she made mistakes. I hope she does answer that question one day.

You are such an inspiration to me in being a loving parent; this will be on my heart today.

Love,
-Mike

4/1/2022

Barbara, Darling,

Today, I woke up at 1 a.m., feeling fully rested. I think meditating has a sleep-like effect. I have read this in some of the books about Buddhism.

Since I had the extra time, I started another audiobook, *Buddhism without beliefs*. I have to take some time to absorb the ideas about talking to kids in the book, so I am taking a break for now. A phrase in this new Buddhism audiobook read, "Creating conditions that are conducive to awakening." Until I read this, I couldn't find the right words for describing why I think we should be a part of, perhaps, a significant part of each other's lives. This is basically why I think we should spend our lives together, perhaps the rest of this life together. I believe we can help awaken one another. We have seen that we have done this for each other to some degree, and I believe we can continuously do this for each other. Maybe you will share this belief. Maybe you already do.

I am learning a lot about not taking things personally and getting to practice what I am often learning from Anthony since he moved in with us. Yesterday, I had an idea or revelation about what ego actually is. It is a subjective construct of the identity we assign to the being that life is experienced through. "Them" is also a construct of an identity we assign to other beings based on "our" being's experience. I will make this diagram to explain some further points:

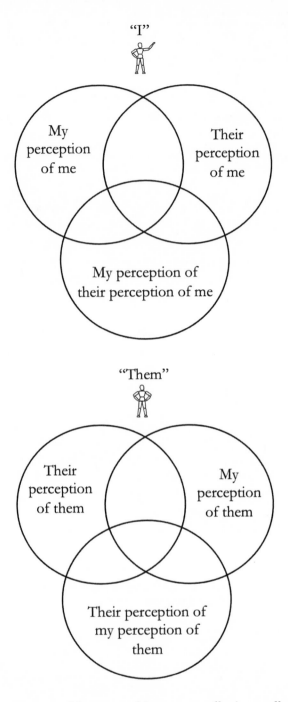

When it comes to taking something personally, it usually happens when areas of perceptions do not overlap, and there are a lot of non-overlapping perceptions to consider. Suppose someone says, "You are dumb," we should consider the following perceptions:

1.   I think I am smart

2.   I think they think I'm dumb
3.   One person may think the other is dumb
4.   One person thinks they are smarter than the other person
5.   One person thinks the other person does not know they are dumb

As you can see, there are many contradictions. The only person who can know what someone actually is or isn't is oneself. Even then, that is still a perception, and if others do not widely hold that perception, much conflict will ensue. The idea of losing one's ego means accepting that we have perceptions but not accepting them as the only perception. It means to believe that our world and existence as we know it is created and formed by a set of overlapping perceptions, but inevitably some perceptions will not overlap. This non-overlapping of perceptions is fundamentally what creates interpersonal conflict and disappointment. If our existence depends on having a perception of ourselves, then an incongruency in what we think about ourselves and what someone else thinks about us is an erosion of our existence. If we can erode our existence and instead view the world as a movie being continuously streamed, when someone says, "You are dumb," we can say, "Oh, that's interesting," rather than "No, I'm not!" If we watched a movie from a first-person perspective and someone said, "You are dumb," are we going to yell at the TV, "No, I'm not!?" Are we not more likely to ask a question, "I wonder why that person thinks that?" If we understand that the construct "I" is created by the consciousness living inside the body it controls, we can dissolve that construct and just watch the movie and enjoy it. Even if we cannot dissolve that construct, we can at least understand that "my perception of myself is not the same as someone else's perception of myself and more importantly, my perception can exist independently of theirs."

Am I dissolving my electron cloud? I'm not sure, but I know I cannot dissolve my sense of me without dissolving my sense of you.

Love,
-Mike

4/1/2022

My Love!

I know I already wrote to you today, but there is a really strong emotion in me to write to you again.

I just got back from the park where we used to go, and it brought me so much joy. What is this love I have where I cannot see you for four months and not talk to you for two months, yet I still feel just as much in love with you now as I did then!? It is eternal love, the love that wraps around every day, every week, every month, and every year forever and ever.

Maybe it will be ten years until I see or talk to you again, like in the movie "The Notebook," but I know I will always love you no matter how long it is. Ten years is a lot less than a million years, and as far as I know, we still live in the same city. That's a lot less than a million light-years apart. We live in the same galaxy, and every day that passes, I am a little bit happier because I know I am a little bit closer to you.

Love,
-Mike

Barb,

I was gonna save this for tomorrow, but thoughts of you keep distracting my attention. My imagination is becoming ever more detailed. I can see you in your blue Japanese nightgown getting ready for bed, but you take a quick pause to come give me a kiss.

In my meditation this morning, I discovered the 4th and 5th dimensions. It's a little complex to explain, but the 4th and 5th dimensions are our perspectives and other people's perspectives, respectively. I'll tell you more about it later. I know it sounds crazy right now.

This afternoon I discovered eight truths of egolessness
1. I am not my perception
2. I am not their perception
3. "I" does not exist
4. Only a perception exists
5. They are not my perception
6. They are not their perception
7. "They" does not exist
8. Only a perception exists

If you practice saying and believing these truths, you will find you do not take things personally and are much less likely to offend or start a quarrel. I have been practicing on Anthony; he's what people call abrasive. The truths work perfectly. When he says, "Why do you act like I'm stupid!?" I remind myself that I am not their perception. They are not my perception. I remain perfectly calm, like someone playing a video game or watching a movie.

I hope these ideas help you interact with anyone in your life that causes you pain with the words they use.

Love,
-Mike

Barbara,

My love, good morning. It is a really nice day out. I guess it rained, or there was a lot of dew because the cushions on my patio furniture are wet. White flowers are blossoming in our neighbor's tree, and the grass is growing pretty fast. Spring is definitely here.

Last night, I went to have dinner in Tulsa at Outback. It reminded me of when I would have dinner by myself in Iowa. I remembered how much I would miss Kristen after being away from her for so long. Towards the end, I couldn't even go a week without seeing her ☺. It also reminded me of when you watched Daniella in July of 2018 on my birthday so Kristen and I could go have dinner at the Outback near your house. Kristen and I had been arguing about something just before we dropped off Daniella. The dinner was not pleasant. I remember that I couldn't wait to leave. I wonder when you last went out with David. I remember when I offered to watch Karen and Victor after we got back. You and David gave a very painful, "Thank you, ok." That was when I realized just how much more unhappy you and David were than Kristen and me. I remember joking with Kristen that there was not much romance happening in your bedroom when we went to Galveston. It was a mean thing to say in retrospect, but it was the basis for my surprise when you told me you "had sex with David a month ago" in the middle of November. I have come to understand something called conjugal kindness, and now I believe I understand how you could have sex with someone you dislike so much. I wonder how much of Kristen's kindness was conjugal. It's funny that I couldn't imagine a relationship where two people would be willing to have sex with each other but not interested in having dinner. Yet, I was in a relationship that was not so different not so long ago. Oh, the misery we bring upon ourselves because of our attachments. If I didn't cry so much already, I would cry, but now there is nothing left to do but laugh. Lol. I need a new acronym to describe that laughing Buddha with the belly, so people understand that emotion you have when you laugh because there are no tears left to cry. "bblol" for Buddha belly laugh out loud.

It's been almost a year since that trip we took down to the river. It was Kristen's birthday; I remember a couple of things from that trip. Kristen was mad at me, and David made some joke about SuperSonic. He also made fun of me for trying CBD in Galveston. It's amazing how much I managed to dislike him in the few times I interacted with him. He once joked that we should make a company that recycled baby poop. He was just mocking my entrepreneurship in general. Together, David and Kristen made the trip to that river very memorable for me. I also remember you coming to ask me what was wrong with Kristen and how concerned you were about her. I imagine part of your reason for staying away from me is for her. Sorry to report to you that she, a year later, is still unhappy, even without you talking to me. And now, like when I went to Michigan, I am happier the more time I spend away from her. It's not that we cannot love each other, but we are not compatible to be everything to each other. I hope she, you, and David can see this one day. I think Kristen and David may resent themselves or us for the rest of their lives because of this fact. It's not my path to live with and be married to someone who cannot accept the facts and incompatibilities in our relationships. It took me eleven years to learn that no amount of time will make people more compatible. We have made children in order to increase biodiversity according to our instinct. Still, it doesn't necessarily mean the person that will create beautiful children is a great person to help us become our truest selves. I have been lifting weights at the gym for eleven years, and I think it's time to take all that strength I have built up via my relationship with Kristen and apply it to something outward in the world. I imagine this is the path you are on. I believe we will lift one another towards this end and accomplish great things once we get past this transition and stop feeling guilty for detaching ourselves from Kristen and David.

Love,
-Mike

4/3/2022

Barbara,

There are so many things I want to tell you, and I'm using a different pen. I have been using the SuperSonic pens, but they are not as smooth as this pen, so they make my hand tired after writing with them for a little while.

Ok, let's see. Ok, to start, I will share this poem I wrote yesterday

> I am not angry though I feel anger
> I do not breathe though I feel the breath
> I do not want though I feel wanting
> I have no sight though I can see
> I am not hungry though I can feel hunger
> I do not walk though I chose where this body steps
> I am not my experiences though I experience
> I am not this construct of existence though I exist
> I am like a player in a simulation
> I feel pain though I do not suffer

I am developing a growing sense of the separation between what I am experiencing right now and all the thoughts inside my head, memories, hopes, and concerns. It's not that there isn't a time for those things; it's just a lot less often than I do them. I think what happens as we grow older is we spend more and more time thinking until we eventually believe we are our thoughts. We develop a philosophy that this dream is part of me or that thing I enjoy is part of who I am, or this person is part of my identity. As romantic as all of that sounds, identifying with things we don't have control over will eventually make us unhappy. We say, "I am a husband or wife," and then our spouse dies or divorces us, and our entire world crashes down. We say, "I am a mother or a father," and then our child dies, moves out, or disowns us, and our entire world crumbles.

The truth is that we create our own grief

We possess things that don't belong to us, and when we feel we no longer possess them, we feel such overwhelming loss. If we want sustained long-term happiness, we have to eliminate these cycles of grief by not attaching ourselves to transient things that we'll eventually lose. Or even better, we have to stop attaching ourselves to anything at all. If we are already attached to things we consider to be part of our identity, we can do ourselves a favor and detach on our own time before we lose them.

It is odd when you meditate and become so aware of your body, so focused on your existence, that the fabric of reality begins to crumble and fade away. I very-quite literally find myself in places that I have not actually been to before in meditation. It makes sense, I guess. You can't get in the car and drive to the store if you are holding onto your kitchen table. We cannot become dramatically different from what we are if we hold onto what we are. This really begs the question, "Why do we need to be anything at all?" I suppose identification helps us navigate a world of identifiers. It's probably better to think of these identifications more like clothes than body parts and walk around naked as often as possible ;-).

This brings me to an observation I have made about what I previously thought was my sexuality and sex drive. For the past couple of years, I have thought that "I am a sexual person," but I think it's more accurate to say, "I really enjoy sex." The difference is that when I don't engage in sexual activity, it doesn't seem to make me unhappy now. It's just that I think if I did engage in sexual activity, I would really enjoy it. The result is an entity that has choices, perhaps even preferences, but can enjoy the present regardless of that present. Yesterday, I was putting down weed killer, and I was totally focused on that, and it was like I was playing a game. I was absolutely happy and really enjoying this rather objectively boring task. It was like, "This is my task right now, and I am doing it, and this is absolutely awesome!"

Why do I have to tell myself, "I am a father?" Am I afraid of myself? Am I afraid that if I don't hold onto this identity, I might not take care of my daughter? I see these three ways of overcoming fear:
1.   Re-assure myself the fear will not be fulfilled
2.   Accept that the fear may be fulfilled and believe I can be happy even if it is
3.   To fear something else more

If my daughter runs into the road, I may jump in front of a car to save her. I feared losing her more than I feared the car, which is 3. Most people choose either 1 or 3, and when 1 is fulfilled, they are devastated. Can we not just say, "I chose to take care of this child as best as possible because this child needs someone to take care of him/her?" I'm not saying we can't or shouldn't make commitments, but there is a huge difference between saying, "I'll play poker with you" and "I'm a poker player." I think we should avoid making hard commitments whenever possible and prefer a shorter time frame when doing so. I can commit to taking care of a child as best I can without telling myself I am doing this because I am a parent. We commit because it aligns with our perspective or that commitment helps us gain better alignment with our perspective.

Lol. I know many things I write seem to or actually contradict one another, but I promise it makes sense to me. When I see you again, you will be able to get a glimpse of the thought process I went through to get to where I am so that we can get to the same place. You wrote, "We are approaching each other." I know you are on your own and separate path right now, and when our paths meet, I will be able to show you where I have been so you can understand where I am going. That way, you can make a better choice when deciding if you will go with me.

Yesterday, David installed Telegram. It didn't mean much other than the fact that things are changing even though I do not know what those things are. Something compelled David to install Telegram. I don't know what, but it wasn't nothing. I am changing so fast I barely understand who I was a week ago. It tells me you and/or he could be changing too.

> Nothing is permanent except change.
> -The Buddha

Each day, I wake up a little bit happier, a little bit closer to the sun, a little bit more beautiful, a little bit more aligned with myself, and a little bit freer. It is, as you said, a "work of liberation," and I am accelerating even faster, letting more and more go. Yet, the freer I am, the more real you become to me. I can feel the width of your wrists in my hands. I can feel your long hair fall across my fingers. I can measure your shoulders with mine. I am more and more confident I will see you sooner than I had thought. And I am so in love with you, but now I am no longer falling in love with you; I am rising in love with you.

Love,
-Mike

4/4/2022

Babe,

Good morning. This morning's meditation was a challenge. I had so many images flashing into my head. It was difficult to focus on my breathing and get into a deep meditative state. I realize some of this is caused by the amount of time I spent on Facebook the last couple of days. I have started to diet, so I don't get the dopamine hits like I used to from food, so I am drawn to get that dopamine from social media. Also, last night when I was falling asleep, I realized I was just feeling lonely. I don't know if it's a temporary thing that will pass like a cloud or something that will grow, but I believe I should continue meditating for thirty minutes at least three times a day for now. If I spend less than that, I find it does not keep me on my path toward peace and self-alignment. I worry more, do less, and move in the direction of misalignment. Like right now, I have so many scattered thoughts and emotions that it is challenging to stay present.

I decided to start a vlog focused on SuperSonic. Maybe this can help create a sense of accountability. I imagine if you were with me, we would be helping each other focus on achieving our goals. Feelings of doubt are presently bombarding me, but the good thing is I can separate my perspective from the emotions. I now try to say "I feel doubt" rather than "I am doubting" because I don't believe the second one is true. We can do really only the following:

- See
- Feel (emotion)
- Decide
    - Speak
    - Think
    - Move our body
- Hear
- Touch
- Taste
- Smell

That is all. We have our five senses plus emotions that offer sensory input, and then we can choose what to think, say, and how to move our body. Everything else just has nothing to do with us. If we imagined a game that added emotions, touch, taste, and smell and added the ability to decide our thoughts (with some practice), this would be our life. A lot of times, really strong emotions can overwhelm our ability to choose our thoughts. But suppose we practice controlling our thoughts in meditation. In that case, we can get to a point where we can feel strong emotions and appreciate them without making choices about what we say or how we move our body that is unhelpful to us and other people, especially ones we care about.

Oh, how much I chose for you to live in my thoughts. Your presence is like a sweet fragrance. I can very much remember your rosy perfume and how it filled the air inside my car as we drove together. As I held you in my lap and let your cheek rest against mine, I have found that balance between enjoying thoughts of you and the kind of wanting that is distracting and creates suffering. The Robin Hood song *Love will Last* plays in my head now. I shift into a state of focus and meditation on you.

I love you very much, Barbara, and I know you love me. I do believe, in reverence, that we were made for each other. I look for no one else. Sure, can we enjoy a relationship with someone else? Yes! But my dear, you make my heart bloom like no other ever has.

Love,
-Mike

Barbara,

The days seem to pass ever faster. I have gotten new pens to
write with, and it definitely feels easier. They feel smoother.
There is a padded grip with little ridges on the grip; they are
called zebra pens. I like them.

There are so many changes I am making from day-to-day. It is
harder to relate to how I saw things just a day ago.

Today, I decided I would start practicing letting go of making
judgements. I started a few months ago to let go of making
simple judgements like "good," "bad," "right," or "wrong." This
is more difficult when a five-year-old is questioning everything
that is said and done, but a lot is learned from her. Using the
words "I," "me," "want," and "should" is also difficult but can be
done.

I decided to explore what life would be like without caffeine. I
have noticed that it increases my heart rate beyond the default
rate. This is fine, but I would like to see what life is like without
coffee. I already noticed I am sleeping less. My theory is that
when someone is not stressed out all day, the body requires less
time to recuperate. I have given up caffeine for like a week before
for a tolerance break, but never longer. I have been drinking
coffee since I was like fourteen years old. After waking up this
morning, I went straight to meditation and started deep
breathing. I wonder about the reason for ever drinking coffee, to
begin with. Can I accept being tired when it is inconvenient? I
wonder if you ever drink coffee. I wonder so many things about
you.

I think more and more of my picture of you comes from my
imagination. I know that whatever picture I have of you now,
based on my imagination and the time we spent together, will be
different from the picture I form about you after I start spending
time with you again. I know that it is different from the picture
you have of yourself.

I would enjoy it very much if you were here in my arms right
now, telling me how you see yourself and the world. Are you
"seeing people as they are" or seeing people as you see them? I

would enjoy kissing you, holding you, undressing you, and pressing our bodies together. I would like it if I could look into your eyes, share stories about our day and laugh together about the pain we are given. I cannot yet imagine that I would not like these things any day from now until I die.

I would like it very much if today was the beginning of those days.

Love,
-Mike

Love,

Where are you love?
I see you flying toward me
I hear you calling to me
You seem earnest and tired
It is time to rest your wings

-Love

4/5/2022

Barbara,

It seems that not taking caffeine is having some interesting effects. I feel more tired. Lol. That is to be expected but being this tired is unusual. This time, it feels almost like a drug. My ability to think is impaired, but my capacity for acceptance isn't. So, I accept that I am impaired. While we do have control of what we think, our control over what we think is not immune to our choices about our bodies. My understanding of the symbiotic relationship between the body and mind has improved through this experience. If we take care of our body with the choices our mind makes, our body will take care of our mind. It's interesting how completely separate the mind and body are yet how connected they are. I can now also clearly distinguish between urges for things like water, food, and sleep from emotions like irritation, loneliness, and hopelessness from thoughts like "I see a fish," "I will write," and "I am feeling tired." These experiences reinforce the notion that what we are is thought and consciousness. The judgments we make about ourselves are choices informed by mostly emotions which ultimately become our ego. So, the difficulty in overcoming our ego can be alleviated if we believe that we are whatever we decide we are. But by making a choice about what we are, whether informed by our perspective or someone else's, we create the ego.

> ...What we imagine we create
> - The Buddha

This may feel empowering to realize that we can create whatever identity for ourselves we are inclined to, but there is a problem with this kind of empowerment. We build up skyscrapers of our self-image, and then when someone else points out a flaw in the foundation, we tear them down, and our self-image becomes rubble, or we deny the observations of others and live in our own very different reality. This is why The Buddha resolved that ego and its creation led to greater suffering. So, to remove the ego, we must make no judgements about ourselves, constructive or destructive. We must resolve to unclassify ourselves. To put a question mark on what we are or to make no characterizations about our choices. We must believe that we are just a camera to remove our ego. We are empowered to make decisions about our words, thoughts, and actions, and we are empowered to not characterize any of those choices.

I think this also means that we could choose to abstain from making the same characterizations about others. This is more difficult because thought itself relies on identifying what something is. To have a thought of "I feel thirsty," we must know what "I," "feelings," and "thirst" are. We must characterize them. So, we will be successful when deciding which things to judge and which ones not to.

I focus my attention now on how I have judged you, the image of you I have created in my mind. I wonder if that construct is necessary. Do you need to be Barbara, the one I love and who loves me? Can you be simply just the reader of this letter? When I write the word "you," could it just mean to the reader? Or does the love I have for you bind these words together in some special way, like how atoms are bound together? At this moment, I believe regardless of what constructs I have created for you, I love you. I love the perspective, the consciousness that is you regardless of what choices it makes.

I love the very fabric of your existence. I am bound to it by love.

Love,
-Mike

4/5/2022

Barbara, Baby,

I am sitting in my living room, eating a salad. It is Tuesday, so
Daniella is with Kristen. It is quiet except for the Bosa Nova
music playing, and I am envisioning us in different parts of the
world together. We are traveling, happy, laughing, and smiling
together. The more I think about sharing the next part of my life
with you in a significant way, the more comfortable I am with
these thoughts.

I think about how I re-arranged my office as a way to show you I
would make space for you in my life. We only really used that
room one night, but that night is not a night I will forget. Falling
asleep with you and talking about our dreams is something I
wouldn't mind doing many times again.

Where will we go!? Prague? Alaska? New Zealand? I would go to
all the places with you.

Egoless love is when you love someone for absolutely no reason
whatsoever. You just do.

Love,
-Mike

Love,

Good morning. Welcome to my favorite part of the day. I think I like this nickname for you, "Love." To me, it represents the essence of what you mean to me. I have searched the deepest part of my existence to discover what I am and what you are. We are two perspectives. We are both completely unique because no two things can be in the same place at the same time. We are points in space along a three-dimensional axis with an angular rotation along three pivot points. To that end, some of what we are are similar because we shared a perspective on something either at an earlier point in time before we met or during the time we spent together.

And look at our circumstances, yet somehow, we became bound in love and by love despite all the resistance we faced, perhaps still facing.

Do we really know why an electron wraps around a proton? We have created a model of "positive" and "negative" charges, but why do these things, whatever they are, draw to one another? At some point, even science has to say, "I do not know." So, we created a model called "love" to explain what we observed about why people cooperate; why they, despite the difficulty, are drawn to one another.

So, to me, the purest kind of love is the kind that is unjustified and perhaps unjustifiable. The kind that when someone asks, "Why do you love them?" the most honest answer is "I do not know."

I'm not suggesting we should remain in the circumstances out of fear of losing something just for the sake of this kind of love. I am saying it is possible to love someone purely and change your circumstances or relationship with them without that love becoming under threat. I am divorcing Kristen in this context. I believe my love for her is as pure as the love I have for you. I change the context of our relationship for many reasons. Still, one of the most important reasons is that she consciously or unconsciously sabotages my relationship with you because she is afraid of losing me. She thinks marriage was supposed to guarantee she would not lose me. Maybe she will have an epiphany perhaps after we divorce and I am still here. Maybe after she sees we are together, and I still love her, she will realize that possession is an illusion, and she does not need to "have" me to share love with me. I think this could take many, many years.

We do not have to let Kristen's path or David's path keep our paths apart. I am moving closer to you, Love. Keep moving closer to me.

Love,
-Mike

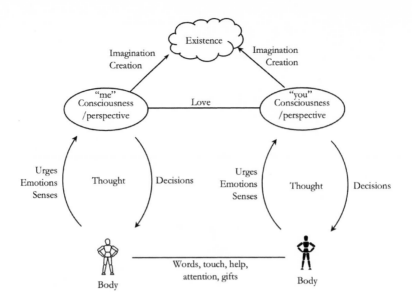

"What we are"

When we make decisions, we do so based on love, urges, emotions, senses, or imagination. But our consciousness itself is not anything. It is the thing that makes decisions and ideas. It is unique only in its position in space and time. When we acknowledge and accept someone's perspective, we acknowledge and accept the very essence of what they are. When we reject their perspective, we reject them. We threaten their very existence. Just because we accept their perspective doesn't mean we agree with it any more than we become someone when we acknowledge their existence. Happiness simply is enlightenment itself. It is an understanding of what the fabric of existence is made of, so you can be happy regardless of your circumstances. No one can take away your understanding. Greater understanding leads to happiness. Love makes us feel happy because another consciousness acknowledges and accepts our own. This process leads to greater awareness which creates happiness.

When we align ourselves, our bodies, our relationships, and our circumstances with our level of awareness, we decrease pain, allowing our thoughts to focus on and achieve the next level of consciousness.

Our old selves are destroyed in this process of transcendence, and we are born from the ashes each time, like a phoenix.

Barbara,

Good morning. Today, my body is a little tired because I was working late last night.

Do you focus on accepting things when you meditate? I accept things I reject, such as pain from others, pain by others, things people do or have done that I don't like, and feelings I have, like the wandering thoughts that appear in my mind while I focus on my breathing. I practice accepting every little thing that life gives me, pleasant and unpleasant, because pleasure is only a matter of perspective.

Yesterday, I told Anthony that the electric bill would be higher than expected, and he had a visceral response. Reflexively out of fear, he rejected this unconsciously, expecting to solicit an emotional response of empathy from me. He acted aggressively when I ate some of his food the day before. I responded by sending him money but didn't argue. I could see he was hoping for a similar reaction from me. This time, I was assertive and let him know that responding this way wouldn't change the electric bill. I reassured him that everything would be ok because people loved and cared about him. I also reminded him he had the option to go live at his old apartment, which is actually more expensive. He lamented that I did not care about him enough to allow him to pay less of the electric bill (he pays 30% of the bills); this confirmed that this was the goal of his animated response. A better response would have been to ask how he was feeling rather than reject his response. It seems that acceptance and curiosity are core aspects of love. Curiosity could also be seen as attention or acceptance without understanding; this makes sense that if love is simply the force that binds two consciousnesses together, then anything which is not based on acceptance is not love. If an electron just simply says to a proton, "I do not reject you in any way," and a proton says to the electron, "I accept you in every way," we can see why they would be drawn to one another. To me, it seems that the same force that binds protons and electrons could also bind consciousnesses together. Love then is not only what binds me to you but also what binds all substances together.

I love you

Love,
-Electron Cloud

Babe,

I had a wonderful experience yesterday evening during
meditation. I had a vision and kind of clarity on what this life is
and why it exists. We are in kind of a simulation, but it is real.
Our consciousnesses do exist outside of each life we live. Before
we take form as an entity on earth, we get to decide which kind
of lifeform we will be. We get to decide which other consciouses
we will meet and interact with. It's like we all get onto a game at
the same time. We are not literally in an elaborate computer,
though. Before earth, there was war, and many cities and
ecosystems were destroyed. Eventually, our species could
transcend corporeal form, and we decided to live our lives in
these kinds of simulations on earth as a kind of game, for fun,
basically. Children are most connected to this goal of fun because
they are closest to original awareness. I think children are most
confused by adults when they are not having fun because they are
aware that fun is the whole reason we live our lives in this form.
They are connected with animals because they know there is a
player inside that animal, a consciousness. Thinking of life as a
game helps to set a better context for why we tend to
automatically feel happier when we are present. When we are not
in the moment, we are not playing the game. We are not enjoying
the game. We hope the game will be different, upset that the
game is not different and neither one of those things will make a
game very fun. By default, if we are present and playing the game,
we are happy because we are having fun.

You and I know each other outside this game, and for some
reason, we chose for our lives to unfold in this way. I wonder
now what we will do next in this game.

Love,
-Mike

4/8/2022

Barbara, Sparrow,

My love for you overcomes me like a tidal wave. I am listening to my heart, and destiny calls me to send you these letters now.

Counting Down the Days (feat Gemma Hays) plays in the background over and over. The vibration of my love for you shakes the room around me, and I do not resist.

-Phoenix, Mike

References

Batchelor, Stephen (Dec 12, 2012). Buddhism without Beliefs. Available from: https://audible.com (Downloaded: 01 April 2022).

Blomqvist, Jan (2014). Time Again. Rent A Record Company.

Böhmer, Ben and Monolink (2018). Father Ocean. Embassy One.

Cayton, Karuna (Feb 1, 2022). The Misleading Mind. Available from: https://audible.com (Downloaded: 09 March 2022).

Hanson, Rick and Mendius Richard MD (Nov 15, 2010). Buddha's Brain. Available from: https://audible.com (Downloaded: 20 March 2022).

Stan, Alexandra (2012). Lemonade. e^2.

Yellowcard (2003). Ocean Avenue. Capitol Records.